The Words that Make Life Work

Daily Self-Talk Messages from the Dean of Positive Self-Talk

Shad Helmstetter, Ph.D., is the author of many books, spanning more than 30 years in the field of self-talk and personal growth, including *What to Say When You Talk to Your Self, The Power of Neuroplasticity,* and the *365 Days of Positive Self-Talk* series. His books are published in more than 70 countries worldwide. Shad has appeared on over 1200 radio and television programs, including repeat appearances on Oprah Winfrey, ABC, CBS, NBC, and CNN News.

You are invited to visit SelfTalkPlus.com.

If you would like to join a worldwide community of positive individuals who are improving their lives with self-talk, you are invited to visit SelfTalkPlus.com. This special self-talk community site features all of the self-talk audio programs which are certified by the Self-Talk Institute. These programs can be listened to on your laptop, tablet, smart phone, or any listening device, as often as you want, anytime you want. This is also the location to meet other self-talkers, attend special self-talk audio and video seminars, be coached by the world's best life coaches, and bring the promise, purpose, and potential of your future to life. Join us!

Visit SelfTalkPlus.com

365 Days of
Positive Self-Talk

for

Finding Your
Purpose

by Shad Helmstetter, Ph.D.

An Inspirational Guide
with Positive Self-Talk Messages
for Every Day of the Year

Includes 'Self-Talk Tips' for Putting Positive
Self-Talk to Work in Your Life
Plus
Special 'Author's Notes' on
Finding Your Purpose

Also by Shad Helmstetter, Ph.D.*

What to Say When You Talk to Your Self

The Power of Neuroplasticity

365 Days of Positive Self-Talk

365 Days of Positive Self-Talk for
Weight-Loss

365 Days of Positive Self-Talk for
Network Marketing

365 Days of Positive Self-Talk for
Recovery

365 Days of Positive Self-Talk for
Self-Esteem

365 Days of Positive Self-Talk for
Meditation & Mindfulness

365 Days of Positive Self-Talk for
Stress & Anxiety

365 Days of Positive Self-Talk for
Successful Selling

365 Days of Positive Self-Talk for
Relationships

365 Days of Positive Self-Talk for
Setting and Reaching Goals

*
Available now or coming soon

365 Days of Positive Self-Talk for Finding Your Purpose

Published by Park Avenue Press
362 Gulf Breeze Pkwy., #104
Gulf Breeze, FL 32561
Copyright 2016 by Shad Helmstetter, Ph.D. / All rights reserved

Helmstetter, Shad
   365 Days of Positive Self-Talk for Finding Your Purpose

ISBN 978-0-9836312-4-8 *Printed format*
ISBN 978-0-9836312-5-5 *Digital format*

Before You Begin . . .

Some starting words to help you get the most from reading this book, and *three secrets you need to know.*

The words you say, especially the words you say when you talk to yourself, not only change your day, they change your life.

This book is based on the amazing scientific discovery that no matter what age you are, your brain continues to change, and that it is *always* changing. Because of your brain's neuroplasticity, your brain is designed to continually rewire itself. And it rewires itself based on the input it gets. That's why your self-talk is incredibly important.

Secret #1:

The thoughts you think and the words you say *physically* and *chemically* change your brain. Your self-talk literally wires your brain to succeed or fail.

Day after day, word by word, your self-talk is wiring programs into your brain. And the picture of you that you wire in most is what you get back out most. *It is your self-talk that creates the foundation for your success or failure in life.*

6

Right now, even as you're reading this, you're wiring and changing your brain.

Your self-talk is the commander of your ship, the director of your life. It is the brain's guiding hand that leads you in the right direction—or in the wrong direction. Your self-talk is the messenger that tells you which path you should follow, what to think and what to do next.

Every thought you think wires your brain to be happy or sad, positive or negative, in a good mood or a bad mood, open to new ideas or closed to them, believing in yourself or not believing in yourself, looking for alternatives or accepting defeat. In fact, everything about you is, at this moment, being influenced or controlled by your self-talk.

What Is Self-Talk and Why Is It So Important?

Self-talk is the direction you give to your brain that tells it how to run your life. Self-talk is everything you say when you talk to yourself. It is your conscious thoughts, and your unconscious thoughts, the thoughts you don't even know you're thinking. It is what you say out loud or what you say silently to yourself. And in its most important form, your self-talk is everything you say or think about *you*—how you feel about yourself—and what you think and what you believe about anything and everything.

Most of us recognize that when we were growing up, we got programmed—and we end up *becoming* those programs and living them out. The remarkable thing, and a great blessing about self-talk, is that you can change that programming. And when you change your programs, you change your life. That's what the *right* self-talk will do for you.

Secret #2:

It's been estimated that as much as 77% or more of all of the programs each of us has right now are negative, false, counter-productive, or working against us.

Since it will always be up to each of us to get rid of the negative programs we have, and replace them with the positive kind, any tool that will help us change them can be a blessing. And self-talk is the best tool for changing our programs we have ever found.

In this book you'll find 365 daily self-talk scripts of the right kind of self-talk—the kind of self-talk we should have been getting in the first place. These self-talk scripts are the result of more than 35 years of studying self-talk and how it works, and writing and recording self-talk scripts in dozens of subject areas.

I first began writing self-talk scripts in the late 1970s. At that time, I was studying self-talk and its effects on personal success, and I was writing the first scripts for recording self-talk audio programs for people to listen to. We had learned that with repeated listening, people could permanently wire positive new messages into their brains, just by playing the recorded self-talk in the background.

At the time, the role that self-talk played in people's lives wasn't yet generally understood. Few people realized that their own self-talk, unconsciously repeated throughout each day, was actually programming their brain, and often in the wrong way.

My studies in this field led to the writing over 20 books on the subject of self-talk and personal growth. My first book, *What to Say When You Talk to Your Self,* introduced the subject of self-talk as we know it today. That book is now published in more than 70 countries, and its popularity shows how mainstream the concept of positive self-talk has become.

My recent book, *The Power of Neuroplasticity,* gives the latest updates on this amazing subject, and presents the science behind positive self-talk. It shows clearly that when it comes to its ability to change our lives, self-talk is based on solid science.

Clear, Positive Programs

In *365 Days of Positive Self-Talk for Finding Your Purpose*, you'll find daily self-talk messages for reprogramming your brain in a clear, positive way.

The self-talk messages have the power to become much more than a few words you read each day. Reading them, rereading them, and wiring them into your brain could do more than just uplift your year—it could uplift your life.

Reading the self-talk messages one day at a time will give you not only daily inspiration, but also a chance to make each day a better day. However, if you're looking for extra guidance or inspiration at any time, turn to any page to see what you find. If you're looking for an uplift, or need to get back on track, you're sure to find the self-talk you need is just a few pages away.

If you want to get the greatest benefit from this book, read each day's self-talk message as you start your day, and read that same message again just before you go to sleep that night.

There's a reason for doing this that has to do with the way the brain gets programmed. Every time you send a message to your brain, your brain *physically, chemically,* records it temporarily. The more positive messages your brain gets, the more positive directions it will record—and in time, with enough repetition, your brain will go beyond recording them temporarily; it will "wire them in," by creating new neural pathways, and act on them.

Each time you read the positive self-talk phrases in this book, you're sending more healthy messages to your brain. The more you repeat these messages, the stronger and more permanent they become. So you're literally rewiring your own brain with healthy, positive thoughts and messages.

Is Positive Self-Talk Telling You the Truth?

When you first read or listen to positive self-talk, because it's positive and stated in the *present* tense, you might think, *"But that's not me,"* or *"That's not true about me."* That's because some self-talk can sound too good to be true. So is it?

The answer is that positive self-talk paints a new picture of how you're *choosing* to become. It may not sound like you or your life the first time you read it, but it defines the new choices you're making to *become* that way. It may not be you at the moment, but it's a picture of you that you're choosing to create.

The brain listens best to directions that are specific and detailed. The better your brain can see it, the better it can help you create it. That's why self-talk is worded in the *present tense*; to give your brain the clearest, completed picture possible of what you want to accomplish. The clearer the picture you give to your brain of who you want to become, and how you want your life to be, the better your brain will physically 'wire it in' and help you get it.

When you see an artist's illustration of the fabulous new home you're going to build, you don't look at the picture of your home and say, *"This isn't true,"* or *"This isn't real,"* just because your dream home isn't built yet. You look at the illustration of that beautiful new home and see yourself living in it! It may not be a touchable reality when you first imagine it, but it is a future reality in the process of becoming real.

That's what positive self-talk is: *it's a picture of you as you choose to become*—the picture of you you're telling your brain to create. The right self-talk is telling you the truth of who you *really* are, and what you choose to do now to bring the real you to life.

The Most Important Key to 'Success' is
Repetition, Repetition, Repetition

Secret #3:

What you repeat frequently, wires the brain. That's so important, it bears repeating: Repetition wires the brain. Because what you experience most, you 'wire in' most, the most important key to success is repetition.

Repetition is the key to wiring or rewiring your brain in the right way because of the way neural networks are formed in the brain. Neural pathways in the brain are formed by repeatedly sending electrical and chemical messages (your thoughts) over the same route—over and over again—like building a highway with layer after layer of concrete or asphalt.

In your brain, each time you travel over the same route—each time your brain receives a repeat of the same message—the pathway becomes stronger and stronger, until, with enough repeated passes, you've created a new 'highway of thought' in your brain.

When similar highways connect, "programs" are formed. These programs—inter-connected mental super highways—become our *beliefs*, our *attitudes*, and our *opinions* about everything. And we create all of them through repetition. Everything we believe, about anything, actually comes to us through repetition. Everything you believe about *yourself*, also comes to you through repetition.

Now, when we want to rewire our brains with better programs, we use the same process. But this time we're repeating better messages—positive self-talk—and building new, more positive, neural networks in the brain.

A message that isn't repeated gives your brain only a passing thought; it doesn't get wired in permanently. But the exact same message repeated often enough, creates a new neural pathway, and it becomes a 'permanent' part of who you are.

Highlight and Reread Your Favorite Self-Talk

When you find a daily self-talk message that you especially like, or one that speaks to you with special meaning, be sure to mark it so you can easily find it and come back to it.

Since the more often you repeat any self-talk message, the more you'll begin to wire it into your brain, it's a good idea to go back to those messages you'd like to make a permanent part of your positive programs, and read and reread them again.

People often learn to recite lines of their favorite poetry by reading them often. Some of the self-talk you'll find here is poetry for a positive mind, and you can learn and remember it by rereading it frequently.

Also, mark any messages you feel could help you at a later time, should you ever need them. Self-talk messages can offer encouragement, a helping hand, and can uplift your spirit when you need it most.

Reading Self-Talk Out Loud

You'll also benefit from reading the self-talk scripts out loud. When you read aloud you're engaging more senses and increasing your brain activity. When you're reading self-talk out loud and focusing on the message you're reading, you'll increase retention. Reading self-talk in this way isn't required to get the benefit of practicing self-talk, but it will help.

If you find reading aloud is not convenient—you may want privacy when you're reading out loud—or if you find it difficult to add to your schedule each day, just read the self-talk in a normal way, silently, to yourself. The most important thing is to read it, and make it as convenient as possible, so you'll have no reason not to stay with it.

Listening to Self-Talk

Along with reading self-talk each day, you may also want to add listening to self-talk to your daily schedule.

By itself, reading self-talk helps you see each day in a healthy way, and reading even one passage each morning and at night is a habit you should create. When you also listen to self-talk each day, it will help you rewire your brain in a stronger way, and it will do it faster.

Positive self-talk was first written and recorded to be listened to. (The first professionally recorded self-talk programs were introduced in 1981.) The idea proved to be so helpful that many thousands of people now listen to 10- to 20-minute self-talk sessions every day on their smartphones or other listening devices.

Recorded self-talk is different from the self-talk you find in this book. The recorded form of self-talk goes into greater detail; it is more in-depth in specific subject areas that are important to you personally, that you want to work on. In recorded self-talk, each self-talk phrase is also repeated three times, each time with different word emphasis and intonations that increase the strength of the message, and help the brain wire it in faster and stronger.

Recordings of subjects like self-talk for weight-loss, personal relationships, health and fitness, job and career, finances, self-esteem, etc., and even special self-talk for kids and young people, give the listener in-depth self-talk programs that are designed to be listened to each day.

When self-talk is listened to frequently—usually each day for two or three weeks on each subject area you want to work on—the daily repetition of the self-talk causes the brain to rewire itself naturally, and with the right programs. The more often your brain hears those same messages repeated, the stronger and faster they are wired in.

You can listen to self-talk programs that are certified by the Self-Talk Institute at SelfTalkPlus.com.

"Self-Talk Tips"

Throughout this book you'll also find useful *"Self-Talk Tips"*—helpful ideas and discoveries that will show you how positive self-talk works, where it comes from and what it can do for you.

Instead of waiting to read each *Self-Talk Tip* until you arrive at its place in the book, you may want to skip ahead and read through more of the tips, just as though you're reading a separate "how to" companion book of tips to help you get the most from the daily self-talk messages.

The importance of repetition in creating positive neural pathways in the brain is so important, that some of the key points will be expressed, in different ways, more than once. If you find a key concept idea that is repeated, that's not an accident. That's how the brain gets it, holds it, and, with enough repetition, wires it in.

"Author's Notes"

Also included in this edition, and featured throughout the text, you'll find a number of *'Author's Notes.'* These notes express my thoughts and insights into the search for 'purpose'—the grand search that I have called *the most important quest of our lives.* It's through these notes that I talk with you 'one on one,' and share my personal thoughts—beyond the self-talk messages—with you.

Enjoy Each Day, and Enjoy the Journey

I hope you'll find the self-talk both uplifting and helpful. And I hope that among the many self-talk messages in these pages, you'll find some of the answers in your quest for the incredible person you were designed to be. To get started, all you have to do is choose a date, go to that page, and let the journey begin.

Author's Notes:
Some Helpful Ideas for Finding Your Purpose

It isn't always easy to find your treasure chest of *purpose* the first time you go looking for it. Here is a short list of such treasures. There are many more 'purposes' that could be on the list:

● *To learn to love yourself* ● *To learn to forgive yourself* ● *To learn to love others* ● *To live your faith* ● *To be creative* ● *To help others* ● *To be strong* ● *To inspire* ● *To invent* ● *To bring happiness* ● *To give guidance* ● *To heal others* ● *To heal yourself* ● *To learn humility* ● *To give aid* ● *To craft* ● *To create beauty* ● *To rescue* ● *To comfort* ● *To forgive others* ● *To question* ● *To practice charity* ● *To protect* ● *To be spiritual* ● *To be a parent* ● *To counsel* ● *To create joy* ● *To practice courage* ● *To create freedom* ● *To make music* ● *To share* ● *To learn healthiness* ● *To be compassionate* ● *To care for others* ● *To practice science* ● *To challenge the norm* ● *To explore and discover* ● *To solve problems* ● *To build* ● *To learn to accept* ● *To teach* ● *To tell* ● *To be part of a team* ● *To learn tolerance* ● *To have vision* ● *To connect with your higher self* ● *To learn to endure* ● *To foster peace* ● *To make a difference* ● *To enlighten others* ● *To learn to give* ● *To learn to receive* ● *To listen* ● *To find wisdom* ● *To learn patience* ● *To learn gratitude* ● *To give hope* ● *To serve* ● *To find meaning* ● *To learn* ● *To grow* ●

You may find more than one of your personal purposes on this list, or your own treasure may not be there. But the list should get you started. Remember: You choose your purpose, and your purpose chooses you.

– S.H.

16

January 1

"Why would I put off a better future when I can start right now? Today I choose to take control of my life, decide what I want to do next, set my goals, put myself into action, and take a clear, strong step forward, into my own, incredible, unlimited, positive future."

January 2

"It is because of my quest, and my questions about myself and my life, that I find the answers. Because I question, I search. And because I search, I find what I'm looking for."

January 3

"I have been given the gift of a life of opportunities to learn, grow, and live up to my best. I am so thankful for the gift, and I prove it every day."

January 4

"By finding my purpose, I also learn which of my talents I need to develop, and which of my skills I need to improve."

January 5

"I am mindful. Throughout each day I am consciously *'aware of being aware'*—of my attitude, my actions, my thoughts, and my words. Because I am mindful, I control the direction of my mind and the direction of my day.

January 6

"When it comes to my goals, the most important thing l can do is to believe in myself. l can set goals, be strong, and work hard, but if l want to succeed, l will have to make the choice to believe that l can."

Self-Talk Tip #1
The Amazing Power
of *Mindfulness*

Being 'mindful' is the art of *being aware of being aware.* There's a good reason for getting good at it. We're not aware of what goes on in most of our brain. Over 90% of our choices are made without our being aware of why we're making them. Most of the brain is working entirely on its own—without our conscious input. (That's where most of our problems come from; our hidden, unconscious programs are in control of most of what we think and do—and most of our unconscious programs are negative.)

When you consciously practice being mindful, you become aware of what you're thinking, and why, and you take back control of your life from the 90% part of your brain that doesn't tell you what's going on. If you really want to be in control, you have to make being mindful the default, and you have to get good at it. Fortunately, with some practice, you can do that.

Since you're reading this book, it won't surprise you to know that one of the best ways to become mindful of what's going on in your brain is to practice using positive self-talk. When you practice talking to yourself in the most positive, self-directing way each day, you become more mindful of *everything* you're thinking. And being *mindful* is where a successful day begins.

January 7

"Of all the things I have, of all the things that are important to me, the one thing I can always count on is me—my heart, my mind, my faith, and my absolute determination to live my life in a positive way."

January 8

"I have great value and an important purpose in life. I'm here for a reason, and my #1 goal is to live for that reason. I think about it, I set my goals, and every day I work at achieving my goals."

January 9

"By having a purpose in my life, I create more value in everything I do. By finding an important path to follow, I add to the value of every step I take."

January 10

"The moment I begin to doubt, I think about the best outcome. The moment I fear, I feel the real strength I have within me. And the moment I think I'm not enough, I remember that I am not alone. With my faith and my undying belief, I am greater than anything that could come against me."

January 11

"I count! I add value to the world around me, the people in my life, and everything I do. I was not born to be 'average' or 'indifferent'; I was born to make a difference. My value as an individual, my thoughts, my feelings, my goals, my words, and my actions all count. And I prove it every day."

January 12

"I choose to be successful in some way every day. I see mistakes as learning, problems as opportunities, setbacks as starting points, and limitations as a chance to grow. Every new day is an open doorway to my unlimited future, and one more day to practice becoming the incredible me I was intended to be."

Self-Talk Tip #2
Can *Anyone* Make Positive Self-Talk Work?

Can anyone practice self-talk and make it work for them? The short answer is yes, anyone can do it; *we're all using self-talk all of the time*—it's just that we're not always using the right kind.

The problem is, using bad self-talk is a habit, and one that most people aren't aware of when they're doing it. And because they don't know they're doing it, they also don't know the harm it's doing them. Day after day, negative thought after negative thought, they're wiring negative attitudes and opinions into their brains. In time, the old adage becomes true: they become most what they think about most.

It's precisely the fact that we use self-talk without thinking about it or knowing that we're doing it, that proves anyone can do it. We're all self-talking already.

Practicing positive self-talk is doing what we've been doing all along, but this time changing the words—and getting it right. Doing that is a habit that can be learned. Once you know about positive self-talk, and how it works, you can practice it for yourself. And *anyone* can do it.

January 13

"I am always aware of signs that point me to my purpose. I think about what I like most about my life, the things I do, and what I like to do most. In them, I find the signs that lead me to my purpose."

January 14

"I know that it is often the smallest things that make me the happiest. So I make sure I appreciate even the least noticeable qualities in my life. The more I recognize them, the more important they become."

January 15

"To find the best of me, I look to my highest potential. And to find my highest potential, I always look to the reason I am here. Knowing that, I always know how to live my life."

January 16

"In my life, who I am and the path I choose, is not in competition with anyone else, or the path they have chosen. Instead of worrying about trying to do better than someone else, I just focus on doing my best."

January 17

"My mind does best when it is constantly stimulated and forced to tackle new obstacles in new ways, and is continually confronted with new ideas, new opportunities, and new possibilities. So I set new goals, love the challenge, and improve my mind."

January 18

"If I had just one day to do what I need to do, I would not stop, I would not wait, I would not fear, and I would not give up or give in. That is the way I see today. I know what I need to do, and I do it."

Self-Talk Tip #3
Which Comes First, Your *Purpose* or Your *Goals*?

The answer to which comes first depends on where you are on your life path. Your 'purpose' is your reason for being here. Your 'goals' are the steps you take to fulfill your purpose. If you already know your purpose, then that purpose can direct everything you do, and your goals should follow.

If you're not yet certain about your purpose, then your goals should come first; and one of your biggest goals should be to find out what your purpose is. Only a few people lay out clear, written goals to find their purpose, identify the action steps they have to take to find it, and actively pursue reaching those goals. People who do, give direction to their lives.

On the other hand, if you know your purpose, it gets easier. When you know the ultimate goal, the lesser goals it takes to get you there become clear, and setting and following them become filled with purpose.

If you have found your purpose, set goals to help you reach it. If you haven't found your purpose, set goals to help you find it.

January 19

"There has never been a better day than today to work for what I want to achieve. There has never been a better time than right now to take action. And there has never been a better moment than this one to let myself know I can do it."

January 20

"Who says I was born with purpose and potential? Who says I can be the incredible person I was meant to be? Who says I can reach any goal I set for myself? Who says I can be the winner I choose to be? Who says all that, and who believes it about me? I do!"

January 21

When I have a goal, I have direction. When I have a goal, I know what to do next. When I have a goal, I set the course for my future. When I have a goal, I win.

January 22

"I choose to be determined, strong, resolute, and unstoppable. I have courage, strength, and conviction. I was born to succeed, and that's exactly what I choose to do. I have what it takes to make my life work, and right now, is a great time to prove it."

January 23

"I know that the only thing holding me back from living up to my true potential, is nothing more than fear. Fear of failure, fear of change, fear of what other people think, fear of the unknown, fear of inadequacy, fear of rejection, or any other fear I have. And I also know that all these fears are false."

January 24

"When I know my direction and path in life, and I have made the choice to reach my goal, there is no one who can stop me or take off course. I am *determined* because I have direction."

Self-Talk Tip #4
How to Make the Day
a *Better* Day

Even when you know your purpose and you're on target to reach your goal, you can still have a day that doesn't work. The next time you have a bad day, or when it seems like nothing is going right, there is something you can do that will help.

Your *attitude* about what's happening, how you feel about anything, is never up to what's happening around you. What *tells* you how you feel about what's happening, is up to you and the attitude you *choose*.

So on the next "bad day" try this: Immediately give yourself positive self-talk that lets you know 1) You're okay, 2) You can get through this, 3) Life, overall, is going to go on—it usually does— and 4) Your attitude is up to you.

When the day looks bad, and some old negative programs are working against you, read a page or two of the self-talk in this book. If you listen to recorded self-talk, choose one of your favorite sessions and listen to it. When you do this, you'll actually be adjusting important chemicals in your brain. The more you read or listen to the right self-talk, the better your attitude will get, and life will once again become worthwhile, and not 'that bad.' And it can happen in just minutes.

When you switch to positive self-talk, not only will you look at things in a more positive light, but you could also feel even better than you did before you had the problem in the first place. When a problem comes up, it's what you do *next*—with your own self-talk—that counts most.

January 25

"I'm never afraid to dream. I believe in the best for my future; I dream it, I see it, I prepare for it, I work at it, I create it, and I make it happen. I choose to live up to the best of my dreams, and I choose to make my dreams come true."

January 26

"I'm not here by accident, I'm here for a purpose. My number one goal each day is to become the me I was destined to be."

January 27

"It's not what I have, or how much I can get from the world, that counts the most. I measure my success by how much I learn, how much I love, how much I grow, and how much I give."

January 28

"I look for ways to improve myself every chance
I get. And because I listen, learn, search, study,
practice and apply, I always build, improve, achieve,
excel, overcome, and win."

January 29

*"I have faith. My spirit, my belief, and my personal strength are
alive and well within me. So I move ahead, believing in the most
positive possible outcome, and bravely take the next step forward
into my incredible future. I have faith, and I am not afraid to live
up to my highest calling."*

January 30

"Who am I? I am the very best of the person I choose
to be. What do I want? To reach every goal I set, in the
most healthy and positive way. Where am I going? Into
a future that is filled with the promise of my own
possibilities. How do I know? Because that's who I am."

January 31

"I have a reason for being. I came here for a purpose. The more I *search* for my reason for being, the more it makes itself known to me, and the more I find it in my life."

Author's Notes:
The 'Spiritual' Side of Life

I have never found a life of great purpose and value, without there being a positive spiritual force behind it. Those whose life scripts include the words: "*I am here for a reason, I am lifted by a spirit that guides me ...*" find the greatest passion and joy in their lives.

Without going into the growing body of research in the field of quantum physics which tells us that 'consciousness' itself affects and determines what happens in our material world, I'll just say that mind, thought, and *spirit* play a profoundly important role in our existence.

Studying individuals over many years, I find that within minutes of meeting someone, whether that person has a spiritual grounding, or a materialistic (non-spiritual) world view. And it is always the person with the spiritual grounding who has the greatest dreams, the greatest potential, and the greatest and most positive path of action to accomplish his or her goals.

Your 'everyday you' and the 'spiritual you' are bound together. Life's '*energy*' ultimately comes from *spiritual* energy. The more spiritual light and energy you bring into your life, the better you will do at finding and living your purpose.

— S.H.

February 1

"I am aware, every day, of the importance of purpose in my life. Because I am aware of my need to know and follow the path that is right for me, I look for it, I find it, and I live it."

February 2

"There is no obstacle I accept that I cannot overcome. There is no goal I choose to achieve that I cannot accomplish. There is no purpose I embrace that is greater than my ability to fulfill it."

February 3

"The most important asset I have is my attitude. With a simple, self-directed change of mind, I can instantly alter how good or bad I feel, the direction of my day and how it will go for me, how well I will deal with anything that happens, what bothers me and what doesn't, how thankful I am, how much enthusiasm I have, and how other people will see me. And all of that will come from my attitude."

February 4

"My life is so much more than a simple reflection of what I see in the daily life that surrounds me. I may live in this world, but, in a very positive way, I also live above it, and beyond it."

February 5

"I do many things well. That means I have been preparing to live my life for something of great value."

February 6

"I never blame others for my missteps. I take responsibility for everything I do. When I've made a mistake, I accept it, I learn from it, and know I will do better the next chance I get."

Self-Talk Tip #5
'Waking Up' to Your Purpose

If you haven't found your major purpose in life, the secret to finding it may be in 'waking up'—not from sleep, but waking up your subconscious mind. That's the part of the brain that stores 90% or more of all your unconscious programs, and it is those programs that keep you living on autopilot—the programs that have been making your choices and running most of your life for you—without you even having to think about it.

Waking up your subconscious mind—becoming consciously 'tuned in' to it—gives you a clearer view of who you are, and what you *really* want out of life. And that can lead to discovering entirely new life opportunities that you may never have thought of.

The immediate question, then, is, *"How do I 'wake up' my subconscious mind?"* Fortunately the answer isn't difficult, but doing it will take some practice. To 'wake up' your subconscious mind, begin by noticing *everything* in a clearly focused way, with great *intention*. Start paying close attention to little things (including your own thoughts) throughout your day—things you may never have focused on before. As an example, listen to music as though you were creating each note. Instead of just passively noticing the sunset, direct your mind to look at each of the colors. Instead of having an idle conversation, literally put your mind in the other person's mind and understand the entirety of what the other person is saying. Use that same level of attention in focusing on *everything* you come into contact with each day.

Practice this intensity of focus with every perception you have, and you'll begin to notice a change in your thinking. Instead of living on 'autopilot,' you will be opening the door to a higher level of your own superconsciousness, and all of the ideas and dreams it has been waiting to reveal to you. Within those dreams resides your purpose.

February 7

"My life is my own, and so are my choices about what I do with it. I not only choose my path, but I also choose every step I take."

February 8

"To always live up to my best, I make sure I'm always mindful of three things: To know who I am; to know where I'm going; and to know what I need to do today to keep me on my path."

February 9

"Searching for my purpose is, in many ways, my search for my very best self. The more I search for my meaning in life, the more I learn about me."

February 10

"Today I choose to look for the positive, practice smiling, do something healthy, learn something new, take some time for myself, and do something for someone else."

February 11

"I choose to do something that has value, lives up to my calling, is positive, fulfilling, helps others, and makes me glad that I'm alive. Even the quest to find it brings me joy!"

February 12

"Today I choose to find my purpose in something small or minor that I do—today. When I can find meaning and my 'reason for being' in something small, I can find it anywhere in my life."

Self-Talk Tip #6

When You're Searching for Meaning, Are You a Positive Self-Talker?

Whether you're just getting started as a positive self-talker, or you've been at it for years, here is a simple quiz that will tell you how well you're doing.

- How often do you notice your own self-talk during the day? Often____ Occasionally____ Almost never____
- Do you edit what you might have said or thought, and replace it with better self-talk?
- Instead of thinking negatively, do you stop, think, and recognize the old programs that cause the doubt?
- Do you consciously work to improve your own self-talk?
- Do you see positive self-talk as a short-term idea for your personal growth, or do you see it as a life-long solution?
- Is everything you say, especially to yourself, stated in the healthiest, most positive, way?

You'll know just from answering those few questions how well you're doing at becoming a positive self-talker. Wherever you stand, just keep practicing the right self-talk. Doing that will create one of the most helpful habits you will ever have.

February 13

"If there's something that's holding me back, I don't just wait for it to go away. I figure out what it is, I take action, and I deal with it."

February 14

"I write a list of those things I truly want to do with my life, and I leave nothing off the list. I write it, I read it again and again, and because I stay with it, I find what I'm looking for."

February 15

"I know that life is incredibly good, and filled with endless opportunities. So every day I look for the good, choose the best, and do every positive thing it takes to reach my goal. My success, in anything I do, is not an accident, it is a choice."

February 16

"I make sure I keep my balance and perspective. When things don't go my way, I let myself know that *I can deal with this, I will get past this, and tomorrow is another day.*"

February 17

"Who says I can't do it? Who says I can't reach my goal? Who says I don't get to live my dreams? If you want to know who I really am, just watch me. I reach my goals. I live up to my dreams, and I make them come true. That's who I am and that's what I do."

February 18

"When I'm searching for my calling, I don't just think of one or two reasons why I might be here; I think of dozens of reasons that show me why I'm needed."

Self-Talk Tip #7

Getting Past Your 'Limitations'

Most of our limitations are in our minds. They come from the thousands of programs we receive in childhood, and then from our own unguarded self-talk—and most of those programs are negative.

It makes sense, then, that to discover what we *can* do and who we *could* become, we first have to get past believing in limitations that weren't true in the first place. But many of our negative programs seem very real, and until we change them, we believe they're true.

When we're looking for our purpose, we tend to look only as far as our limitations will allow us to see. Those imagined limitations are like fences that surround us, too high to see over, and with no way to get to the other side. That's why when we think about doing something special with our lives, something important, we often don't believe it's possible—instead of seeing the opportunities, we see the fences.

The key is to recognize that most of your 'fences' are illusions; most of your limitations are only imagined limitations, placed in your mind by negative programs that are not true. Together, you and your positive self-talk can get rid of the fences. And through the power of positive repetition, you can replace your fences with a future of unlimited possibilities.

February 19

"Okay world, get ready! I'm here, I'm prepared, I'm filled with energy and enthusiasm, and I'm going for it! You might as well be on my side and help me get there, because with you or without you, I've made the positive choice to win!"

February 20

"I never let any of my 'limitations' stop me or hold me back. I know that I have the ability to reach any goal I set, and there is no limitation that can stand in the way of my success. After all, I created my limitations in the first place, and I can let them go."

February 21

"By creating the dream in my mind, I make it happen in my life. I follow the simple steps of: dream, goal, plan, action, perseverance and achievement. That's the way success works. That's the way I choose to make my life work."

February 22

"The more times I think the thought, the more I program the message in my mind, and the more I create it in my life. So I always think and repeat good, healthy, positive thoughts."

February 23

"In the midst of my dream, I remember my goal. In the midst of my goal, I remember my plan. In the midst of my plan, I remember my task. In the midst of my task, I remember my day. In the midst of my day, I remember the moment. And in the midst of the moment, I remember my dream."

February 24

"When I think of doing something that brings me joy, while it also brings good to others, I pay attention. That's always a sign I'm on the right track, and closing in on my quest."

Self-Talk Tip #8

Finding the *Incredible You*

As you read the positive self-talk messages in this book, there is something you should know about you: *You were born to achieve.*

You were born with unlimited promise and potential. No matter what has happened in your life up to now, the potential you were born with has never gone away. It may have gotten covered over for a time with the experiences and the difficulties of life, but the incredible person you were born to be *never* goes away.

Old, negative programs in the brain make us believe that we are not capable, not good enough, or smart enough, or talented enough, or destined enough—but all of those programs are wrong.

You have, today, everything you need to make your life work in an exceptional way. If you wonder if that's true, that's just the old, out-of-date, negative programs trying to convince you otherwise.

Do this: Practice positive self-talk. While you're practicing, ask yourself the question: *Would I like to be the person that my positive self-talk is showing me?*

If that's the person you want to be, and if you continue to talk to yourself in the most positive, believing way, your life is going to change. The change will be glorious and amazing. *You will be finding the incredible you you were born to be.* And you will have brought it all to life with your dreams, your belief, and your self-talk.

February 25

"When I ask myself the question, *'What am I doing with my life today?'* I always know the answer. I am thinking up, being certain of who I am, sure of what I want, helping others, reaching my goals, and doing everything I need to do to make life work . . . today especially!"

February 26

"I choose to create balance in my life. Along with my goals and my determination to take action and make each day count, I also practice having patience, staying calm, creating serenity and peace of mind, and making my day a quality day in every way."

February 27

"I am creative. My only limits are those I accept for myself. When I think, I think positive and possible. When I dream, I dream fearlessly beyond. And when I *do*, I do those things that make my ideas come to life. I am creative, and I love creating good things."

February 28

"I am responsible for my place, my choices, and my direction in life. I know that what I make of myself, and what I make of my life, is up to me. So I set my course, I make good choices, I follow my path, and I take personal responsibility for every step I take along the way."

February 29 (Leap Year)

"Even the fact that I am searching for my purpose proves I have value in my life. If I did not have an important reason for being, I would not be looking for it."

Author's Notes:
Your 'Purpose' and Your 'Passion'

Your *purpose* could be defined as your reason for being. Your *passion* could be defined as that which you love doing more than anything else. It's when these two come together in our lives that we find the greatest sense of fulfillment.

My dear sister and mentor, Sylvia, is an artist whose passion is creating wonderfully unique crafts, often from everyday items and materials, such as repurposing plastic containers into beautiful ornaments and flowers; she is able to make beauty from anything. The *purpose* she has dedicated herself to is helping women who have gone through difficulties, improve their self-esteem and self-image. In living to her purpose, for many years Sylvia has volunteered her time to conduct arts and crafts workshops at a well-known women's addiction recovery academy where women are finding a new sense of self, and new futures. (By creating beautiful objects, the women are able to see the beauty they have within themselves.)

As with Sylvia, when purpose and passion are brought together, a natural and positive synergy is created, giving more life and value to both your purpose and your passion. The two don't always have to perfectly coincide, but since you have a choice in choosing each of them, it's a smart idea to look for the opportunities in front of you that bring both of these great energies in your life together.

– S.H.

March 1

"I don't mind if it takes time to find the answer to my purpose in life; it is the most important question I will ever ask. I am excited to do what it takes to find my place in the exciting future I came here to live."

March 2

"I choose to believe. Along with my spiritual beliefs, and the faith I have in the promise of the future, the one belief I have that will always direct my life for the better is the belief I have in myself. When it comes to seeing the best in myself, I choose to believe."

March 3

"I never listen to those who believe we are designed to be average and live without purpose. It is my destiny to be far *above* average and live with *great* purpose."

March 4

"It's my turn to stand; my time to shine. It's time to do what I came here to do, and become the person I was destined to be. So I gather my courage, fortify my strength, and step forward with enthusiasm into my incredible future."

March 5

"I have great value. I have exceptional worth. I have many positive qualities. I have a reason for being, and purpose in my life. I count, and I make a difference. That's me. That's what I choose to accept. And that's how I choose to be."

March 6

"Every day I learn something that helps me grow. I know that just one idea, one good thought, one possibility that comes my way, can change my life for the better. So each day I look for every new idea and every positive thought that will help me become the winning person I have chosen to be."

Self-Talk Tip #9

Purpose and *Patience*

It can be frustrating to feel strongly that there is an important reason you're here, but not have a clear idea what that reason is. If you feel that way, you're not alone. Many people sense they're here for a purpose but don't really know what that purpose is.

There are two steps in dealing with this. The first is to immediately begin programming your own brain to actively start the search. The self-talk you're reading here each day is designed to wire your quest into your consciousness, but it's also wiring your brain to sift, sort, and search through the thousands of programs your brain has already stored for you that may contain hidden clues that will lead to your answer. With the right self-talk, your brain goes into automatic *active* search mode.

The second step is to program in the right amount of *patience*. Great truths sometimes come in a flash of inspiration, but finding a worthwhile and enduring purpose can take time; after all, you're looking for something within you that could be life-changing in many ways. Each day, continue searching and questioning, and each day add the self-talk that says, *"I choose to search for my greatest purpose, and I choose to have the patience to find it."*

March 7

"Who am I, and what can I do? I am a non-stop, go-for-it, confident, upbeat, positive, self-believing, super-achieving, always caring, dream-sharing, uplifting, forward thinking, future-building, life-embracing, success-creating go-getter with unlimited potential and endless opportunities in front of me. That's who I am, and just watch what I can do!"

March 8

"It's not what I fear; it's what I have the courage to face. It's not what I've missed; it's what I have the vision to see. It's not what I cannot do; it's what I'm willing to achieve. It's not who I'm not; it's who I choose to be."

March 9

"I don't complain, I fix it. I don't regret, I build. I don't fear, I get strong. I don't wait, I take action. And I don't stop, I begin."

March 10

"How do I make my life work? I care about others, I believe in myself, I make sure my attitude is always up, I believe in the future, I set clear goals, I'm willing to work for what I want, I always have faith, and at the end of each day, I always know what I want to accomplish tomorrow."

March 11

"I make sure I am mindful of even the smallest things that inspire me, lift me up, and bring me joy. It is within my joy that I find my purpose."

March 12

"I know the secret to living at my best: The more I live up to my purpose in life, the better I do, and the better my life works."

Self-Talk Tip #10

What *Stops* Us From Finding Our Purpose?

When we can't see our purpose clearly, it's usually because our old programs—the limiting kind—won't let us. We grow up being programmed with many messages that tell us what we *cannot* do instead of what we *can* accomplish. Because of this, it is 'natural' that we believe, that *others* may be set up to live out important destinies in their lives, but *we're not*. That's completely false of course—just bad programming that most of us have at least some of—but it *seems* real, even if it's not.

The result of living with the wrong programs is that we form our beliefs of what we cannot do in life, and then base our choices on those false beliefs. We not only become convinced we're not as capable as someone else, we can even quit trying to get better, with the unconscious *negative* self-talk that reminds us, *'Why even bother?'*

No matter how awesome you may already see yourself as being, it's a good bet that you have not yet come close to knowing your true promise and potential. The more you practice thinking 'up' to your true potential, the more your ultimate purpose will reveal itself, and the more you'll recognize the real you.

March 13

"I think about my many positive values every day. I think about my purpose, and I think about all the good I can accomplish while I am here."

March 14

"Today is the day I decide to go for it. Today is the day I set the goal. Today is the day I make the choice to make it happen. Today is the day I put myself into action. Today is the day I do it."

March 15

"When I have doubts, when I'm unsure about what to do next, I always remember to focus on my goal. I review the steps I need to take, make the choice to take action, believe I can do it, and take the next step."

March 16

"I choose freedom. Freedom of thought, freedom of vision, freedom of purpose, and freedom of my dreams. With an unlimited mind, and my unstoppable spirit, a willingness to work for what I want, and the determination to stay with it, I know that I can achieve anything I choose."

March 17

"I practice *dreaming* and *believing*. I dream about my life and my future. And I dream about what I really can do with my life—as long as I *believe*, and as long as I *dream*."

March 18

"If ever I doubt my value, my purpose, or my reason in life, I stop, think about it, ask myself why I am here, and listen for the answer."

Self-Talk Tip #11

With Positive Self-Talk, *You* Choose a Future that Works

So much of the story of positive self-talk is filled with hope. Here's an example:

Is it possible that you get to choose your future, and make it a future that works? According to research in neuroplasticity and self-talk, that's exactly what you get to do. It's not where you've been or what's happened in your life up to now that will write your future—it's what you choose to do next, and the self-talk you use that will get you there.

Many people go through their entire lives believing in the old programs that tell them their destinies are mostly set, and there is little they can do about it. They are taught to believe that luck and the whims of the world around them, are the most important determinants of what happens to them—as though they are pawns in a game of chance over which they have no control.

But breakthroughs in the field of neuroscience tell a different story. We now know that much of what happens *to* us is the result of programs in our brains that literally set us up for success or failure, in almost anything we do.

The result of the research is that we now know our futures are not solely up to the whims of the world around us. You get to choose a better tomorrow, make sure you have the mental programs that will take you there, and create a future that works.

March 19

"l am not given a 'passing' or a 'failing' grade in life. l am graded only by my own acceptance of myself, and how well l am doing in the life l have chosen."

March 20

"One of the most important things I can do to ensure that I am on the right track, is to always be mindful of what I am doing, where I am going, and *why.*"

March 21

"It's not where I came from, what I have done, what I have or don't have, the difficulties of my past, or what I missed out on, that counts the most. The one thing that counts the most is the attitude I choose to have right now, and what I choose to do next."

March 22

"I have many positive goals in my life, but I know that underneath all of them is a driving force that binds them together. That force is my primary purpose in life."

March 23

"I have decided to be my #1 *believer*. I know that people who make the choice to believe in themselves, always do better than those who don't. So every day I choose to believe in myself and work at improving myself in some way. Each day I do this is a day that works."

March 24

"Every great book and every wise person who speaks of success all tell me that my success will always get down to how much I believe in myself. If that's true, and I believe that it is, then my success in this life, and in this moment, is truly up to me."

Self-Talk Tip #12

The *Purpose* of 'Finding Your Purpose'

There is a huge benefit to finding your purpose in life. Yet, only a small percentage of people focus intently on finding theirs. Their lives are taken up by working for an income, raising families, having social interaction, and if there's some time left over, doing something for themselves. The idea of finding purpose is usually left for an occasional subconscious nudge from a forgotten dream, or a soon-forgotten New Years's resolution, and then it's right back to the daily routine of life.

Finding your purpose has a far greater value than our culture assigns to it. Imagine having two small boats—either of which could represent your life. One boat has a rudder, and you can steer it. The other boat has no rudder, and it can only go where the current takes it. If you were to ask anyone which of the two boats they would choose, most people would choose the boat they can steer—in spite of the fact that most of them seem to be riding through life in boats that have no rudder, and are steered almost entirely by the events and the currents of life around them.

When you find your purpose, you have a boat with a rudder—and your direction, day by day, choice by choice, is up to you. You get to go where you were intended to go in the first place.

March 25

"I know that people who have little belief in the future see life as difficult, filled with problems, without opportunity, and nowhere to go. But because I practice believing in myself and in my future, I know that my life is full of opportunities, I can achieve anything I choose, and I have everywhere to go."

March 26

"I remember the dreams I had of who I wanted to be, and the things I wanted to do with my life. No matter how much time has passed, and what has happened between then and now, I still choose to have my dreams, and I choose to bring my dreams to life."

March 27

"I am a seeker and a searcher in every positive way. I search for, and find, the best of myself, and I seek to find the best in everything that I do."

March 28

"I have qualities and talents that I don't even know about yet. I have a goal to discover all of my gifts and bring them to life."

March 29

"I can reach any goal I put my mind to. If I *choose* it, I *do* it. Finding my greatest purpose and reason is a goal I choose to achieve."

March 30

"It isn't only what I dream about that counts. If I want to make something happen, I also set a real goal. I write it down. I identify the obstacles, I write out the action steps, and I get started. My dreams count, but it's the goals I write down, and take action on, that makes them happen."

March 31

"Three important questions I ask myself are:

'If I could do just three things with my life, what would those three things be?'

'If I could do just two things, what would those two things be?'

'If I could do just one important thing with my life, what would it be?'"

Author's Notes:
When Should You Choose Your Purpose?

When, exactly, should you identify the path to find your destiny? When you're very young? When you're middle aged and figuring things out? Or when you're older and wiser?

The answer is now—whatever your age. We, as humans, are actually very good at setting ourselves up for the next 'upward' steps we're supposed to take in our lives. It's as though there is a part of our consciousness that, given the chance, takes better care of us than we sometimes do ourselves. It's our 'higher' self, the wiser part of who we are that taps us on the shoulder and gets us ready for change—and it says to us: *'It's time to move forward, time to learn some new things, time to grow.'*

If you're reading this, it's probably your time to choose your purpose. Or review your past purpose. Or find a new direction. Whatever brought you to these pages at this time, it's a good indicator that you're ready to benefit from your next step—and you're ready to move forward.

– S.H.

April 1

"Of all the days I have lived before, of all the days that lie ahead, now is the time to live my dreams, give life to my greatest goals, and live up to the incredible me I was born to be. And the wonderful, positive, promising, and unlimited world I have in front of me, all begins with me, today."

April 2

"I have a purpose and a reason for being. My path, my calling, is mine to find. It is within me and waiting for me to bring it to life."

April 3

"Right now I choose to change my life for the better. With every choice I make, I am creating the successes I'm living today, and the future I will be living tomorrow. In everything I do, I choose to find my best."

April 4

"The opportunities of this life are unlimited. I have endless possibilities; unlimited things to do. And I'm really enjoying searching, discovering, and doing."

April 5

"I know that people who achieve, first choose to believe. So I make sure that my attitude is up, positive, optimistic, confident, and going for it! Today especially, I choose to believe in myself, and believe in the winner that I am. I can do it, and I know I can!"

April 6

"I plan my learning carefully. I choose to be a quality educated person, but I especially focus on learning those things I need to most successfully fulfill my purpose in life."

Self-Talk Tip #13

Positive *Self-Talk* is More Than Positive *Thinking*

Positive self-talk isn't just about positive thinking; it's about managing *all* of the thoughts that are being wired into your brain.

Unlike basic 'positive thinking'—looking at the world in a generally positive way—positive self-talk could be compared to the flight program the navigator types into the onboard computer on an airplane. Whatever direction the navigator types in is the direction the plane is going to fly: course, altitude, speed—everything the airplane's onboard computer needs to know to take the plane safely to its destination. It's not just a positive thought or two—*it's a detailed set of program instructions that will fly the plane to its objective.*

Positive thinking, by itself, is a good thing, and it helps you look at the world in a bright and healthy way. But positive self-talk, like the navigator's instructions to the computer, is more specific. The right self-talk identifies every step you need to take to get where you're going, sets the course to get you there, keeps you uplifted and motivated on the journey, and makes sure you arrive safely, and on time.

April 7

"Today I get a clear picture of who I want to be. I decide what I need to do to improve myself in some way today, make the choice to do it, and make sure that every choice I make today, will help me become the incredible person I want to be tomorrow."

April 8

"Why do I feel so good about my future? It is because I choose to live with courage, strength, and an unstoppable belief in my ability to imagine the best, overcome challenges, and make things work."

April 9

"Living my purpose each day is what creates the greatest happiness in my life. Living my purpose is loving my life."

April 10

"I keep my mind open to the many options in front of me. Finding my purpose starts with discovering my *options*."

April 11

"It all gets down to what I believe about me. If I think I can do it, I can. If I believe I have it, I've got it. If I really want it, I go for it! If I truly believe in me, I'll prove it!"

April 12

"I see change as a natural part of life, the next pathway to my positive future, and the opportunity to grow. In any change that comes my way, I look for the opportunity in the change, I find a way to learn and grow because of it, and I make it work"

Self-Talk Tip #14
Seeing the Glass as Half *Full*

Behavioral researchers have shown that when it comes to your goals, you only reach what you can see. Or, put another way, you only reach the goals you can clearly imagine. That's true of the biggest and the smallest things in life. Overall, if your brain can't 'see it,' you probably won't get it.

The 'glass' is, of course, a metaphor for what we believe or what we imagine to be. Since the brain will work hardest at helping you get those things that you can most clearly imagine, if your glass is 'half empty' and you can't see the possibility of getting what you want, your brain won't help you get it—*you're wiring your brain to believe it won't work.*

Seeing the glass as half empty stops you from seeing the opportunities that are in front of you, and programs your brain to act as though you won't get what you want. The result is, you usually won't.

When you practice seeing the glass as half full, you literally switch on the part of your brain that searches for alternatives and possibilities. So instead of your brain being busy being negative—and making sure something won't work—when you change your brain to think in the positive, it gets busy looking for ways to make it happen.

April 13

"When it comes to my goals and my dreams, I let nothing or no one take them from me. I hold the key that opens the door to my own unlimited future. That future is mine. What I do with it is up to me."

April 14

"A perfect description of me would include the words *positive, strong, sincere, kind, caring, believing, goal-oriented, intelligent, energetic, full of life, and determined to live up to my best.* That's me. That's the person I choose to become. That's the way I was born to be."

April 15

"I choose to dream, to believe in, and to create, the most remarkable, positive future for my world and for the life I'm living. I am practical and down to earth, but I also choose to dream, and when it comes to creating my own future, I always imagine the best, create the best, and believe in the best."

April 16

"I am here for a reason. I have a job that I came here to do. I may spend time dealing with my day, but I always add value to each day by remembering I am here for a purpose."

April 17

"The reason I wonder, the reason I search, is that my life has a destiny that is mine to find. I love the search, and I know I will love my discovery, and the amazing future in front of me."

April 18

"Right now is a great time to make the choice, gather my energy, fine-tune my focus, get a clear picture of what I want to accomplish, decide to do it, smile, say *yes!* to myself, take a deep breath, and go for it!"

Self-Talk Tip #15
You Were Born to be Successful

Negative self-talk tells us that we deserve *less* than the best. When it comes to love, money, talents, skills, luck, job promotions, good looks or almost anything we'd *like* to have, but may not think we can get, it's our own negative self-talk that's telling us what we don't deserve.

The truth is a different story. You were born to succeed. All of us were. No exceptions. You were designed to excel. Like the flowers of the field or the birds in the sky, one is not created to succeed while another is created to fail. When it comes to life itself, we were designed in every way to grow, learn, overcome challenges, become stronger, and reach the highest levels of personal growth and fulfillment. That's true of all of us.

Blessings aren't handed out randomly or unfairly— more for some and fewer for others. Blessings are given out in direct proportion to *our intention of receiving them, our willingness to work for them, and our willingness to believe in them.*

The real you, the true you that you were born to be, deserves every blessing you choose to imagine and accept. And that gets down to your self-talk and your beliefs about yourself. You will accept and create what you believe you deserve.

Check your self-talk. Make sure you've got the right programs of self-worth and deserving. When it comes to how much you deserve, no matter where you've been or what has happened in your life so far, you were born to have an equal share in the universe. You still have it.

April 19

"My day today is up to me! So l choose to fill my day with high energy, have a great attitude, know that things are going right, and create a positive outcome in everything l do. My day today is up to me, and l choose to make today an incredible day!"

April 20

"I never let problems or challenges hold me back or stop me. Instead of letting problems get me down, I keep myself up! I remember my purpose, keep my eye on the goal, take the right action, believe in the best, have faith, move on, and make my day a winning day."

April 21

"I don't need someone to give me my purpose, or to live it for me. All I need is a dream I believe in, a goal to achieve it, the enthusiasm to give it life, the decision to take action, and the determination to make it happen —and I will find my purpose in my dream."

April 22

"I don't wait for success to just 'happen,' or quietly 'hope' for good fortune to come my way. When it comes to my success in finding my purpose in life, I choose it, I create it, I go for it, and I make it happen."

April 23

"I never let the problems, troubles, or unrest in the world we live in get me down. Every day I am aware of my purpose, I work on my goals, and I believe in the best outcome in everything I do. I make sure my attitude is always up, look for the bright, and find the good."

April 24

"Today I choose to have a great attitude! How I feel about today, and what I do with it, is really up to me. So I choose, right now, to have an incredibly good attitude, feel great about myself, decide to go for it, and make today one of my best days ever!"

Self-Talk Tip #16
The Right Self-Talk Will Help You
Find Your Purpose

If you haven't yet completely defined your purpose, the self-talk you choose can play a big part in helping you find it or create it.

By repeatedly letting your brain know you're searching for a specific answer, your own subconscious mind becomes wired to *look* for that answer. If, each morning, as an example, you use the self-talk that says, *"I am searching for my purpose and I am finding it,"* your brain will actually help you in your search. Because your brain is designed to do what you most often tell it to do, if you tell it to search for your purpose, it will.

When your brain is 'on alert' to help you find your purpose, it will begin to show you new possibilities; it will help you notice things you might not have noticed before; it will start you thinking about your quest in creative new ways; and it will keep you mindful of your goal and keep it's importance in front of you.

Since you get to choose all of the self-talk you use, try this: add self-talk for finding your purpose to your day every day. You may be amazed at the purpose you find.

April 25

"I am not alone. I have my life, my dreams, my goals, and my determination to succeed. And I make sure I always surround myself with my undying faith, others who believe in me, and an unstoppable belief in myself."

April 26

"I have vision. Every day I practice seeing 'the big picture' —how life works, and what I can do now to make my life work best. So I choose to have vision. I see the future I'm creating, and I see a future that works."

April 27

"I know the great truth: that my life, and what I do with it each day, is up to me. I know that I alone am responsible for what I think, what I do, and what I say, and I practice being in control of my life every day, in every positive way."

April 28

"I take time to improve myself, and I work at getting better at anything I do. I may be doing okay so far, but just watch me. Because I'm working at improving myself in some way every day, I will become even better tomorrow."

April 29

"I don't just hope to find my greatest purpose and meaning; I search for it, I pursue it, and I am determined to find it and bring it to life."

April 30

"The value of my life is not based on all of my accomplishments. They're good and positive, but the value of my life is based on how much I accomplish of what I really came here to do."

Author's Notes:
Finding Your Purpose Changes Everything

If life were about 'getting by,' then having a purpose would not be essential. You could just *get by.'* But it's clear that life, and our reason for living it, goes far beyond just getting through it.

Imagine two people who are equal in almost every way. One of them has no real direction in life. He isn't aimless, but he isn't a big goal-setter, either. He gets by. He does okay, has a decent life, doesn't cause problems, and lives an average existence. He doesn't spend a lot of time thinking about his purpose or what he *could* have done with his life. But he gets through it. And one day he dies.

The other person is markedly different in that he has a clear picture of his *purpose*. Instead of just going along with the crowd or settling for average, he knows what he's here for. He sets goals and works at reaching them. He is excited about the future and he has a reason to be positive. He lives life by *choice* and not by *chance*. Instead of being a victim, he directs his own life, and at every turn he is guided by his purpose. Instead of just getting through life, he excels at living it, and he does so every day he is here.

The difference in the lives of those two people, who once were equal, began to take place the moment one of them made the choice to find his purpose and follow it.

— S.H.

May 1

"Today I choose to be at my best and make my day work in every positive way. Today I'm completely in touch with who I am, what I want, and where I'm going. Today is a day I move my life forward. I know what I want to accomplish, I take action, I go for it, and I get it done!"

May 2

"The conscious choice to look for my purpose each day makes me aware of the richness of my life in so many ways. Today, again, I choose to be aware of how good my life really is."

May 3

"I listen to the quiet voice within me that believes in me, encourages me, and guides me. It tells me I am here for a reason, and there is purpose in my life, and it is showing me the path to follow."

May 4

"My personal growth is important to me. I believe in doing everything I need to do to improve myself and make my life better. I choose to learn more, see farther, work smarter, rise higher, and achieve my best in every important area of my life."

May 5

"If I want to make something of myself, it's up to me. It's not other people's doubts that count; it's my belief in me. It's not the challenges I face each day; it's my determination to overcome them. It's not the lack of opportunities in front of me; it's my willingness to find them. My success is not up to the world around me, or up to someone else; my success is up to me."

May 6

"I know there is more to life than endless days and just getting through it. I know there is great meaning, wonderful opportunity to grow, and many chances to be the me I was intended to be."

Self-Talk Tip #17

Do Your *Programs* Measure Up
to Your *Purpose*?

What if your were sent here to live your lifetime doing something of great value? But what if the programs you got while growing up hid your *real* potential and purpose from you? What if your programs don't measure up to your purpose?

That's exactly where most people spend most of their lives.

Our objective is to excel personally; to reach an important target of value in life. But along the way we receive so many of the wrong messages that get wired into our brains, that we not only lose sight of the goal, we don't even know there *is* a goal, a *greater* goal, the reason we're here. And yet, the moment you stop and ask yourself the question, *"What is my purpose,"* there is a part of you that knows, deep down inside, that not only do you have a purpose, but you also desperately want to find it and live it out.

The answer is to first recognize that you have great value, an important purpose and a reason for being, (you didn't come here by accident), you have a job to do, and it's time for you to override any previous programs you got that were negative or wrong. The next step to recovery is to practice changing your self-talk to the right kind—the kind that shows you who you are, and why you came here in the first place.

May 7

"Each day I awake, I recognize that I have another day to live up to my best, bring out the remarkable person that lives within me, and take another step forward on my journey of positive discovery."

May 8

"I choose, forever, to remove the fear that I might not 'measure up' to someone else. I never measure my life by the expectations of others. I live my life based on my own positive expectations to live each day in the very best way. And every day, I measure up to me."

May 9

"I find myself in my joy. I find myself in my enthusiasm for living. I find myself in my goals and in my dreams. And I find myself in the path I choose to follow."

May 10

"I take the time to find the quiet, and in the stillness, to listen. When I listen carefully, and with patience, I begin to get a clear picture of the incredible me I am meant to be."

May 11

"There is no problem I cannot conquer, there is no challenge I cannot overcome. I have been given every talent and ability I need to succeed in anything I choose to achieve. If I want to do it, I can do it. And if I want to make it happen in my life, making it happen is up to me."

May 12

"I know that the real secret to my success gets down to my perseverance, my undying persistence, and my absolute determination to reach my goal. So I start, I stay with it, and I keep going. And because I will not give up, I reach the goal. That's how I think, that's how I live, and that's how I win."

Self-Talk Tip #18

How Is Your Self-Talk? Are You Getting It Right?

All of us talk to ourselves all of the time. Until we focus on our self-talk, we're usually not aware of it. Without really thinking about it, we're either carrying on a running conversation with ourselves, or we're telling ourselves something—and what we're saying may be more complaint than truth.

All of our self-talk, conscious or unconscious, is helping to wire or rewire our brains. And most of our self-talk is the negative kind. That can literally wire your brain in the wrong way—with negative self-talk—which is the #1 reason most people fail to reach their highest potential in life.

Most researchers on the subject agree that there are two main reasons why so many people get their self-talk wrong:

The first is that most people aren't aware that their self-talk physically wires neural pathways into their brains. Those pathways form their beliefs about everything. The second reason most people get their self-talk wrong is because they didn't learn how to change it; science is just now showing them how to get it right.

The big positive in all of this is that once you know what self-talk is and how it works, it isn't hard to get it right. When it comes to self-talk, practice makes perfect.

May 13

"Each day is another chance for me to restart my life—with promise, opportunity, and unlimited potential. No matter where I've been until now, I have the most important part of my life in front of me, and I'm just now getting started."

May 14

"I am curious, inquisitive, and full of questions about me. The more I learn about myself, who I am, and what I want to accomplish with my life, the more I like the person I'm choosing to be."

May 15

"I have, spirit, I have faith, and I am blessed in so many ways! I am filled with life, full of hope, and determined to live up to my greatest potential."

May 16

"Instead of fearing the future, I embrace it. Each day in front of me is a chance to learn more about myself and the incredible journey I'm taking. I love the future and I'm making it great!"

May 17

"Today I choose to be strong, confident, sure of myself, and unafraid. I know what I'm going for. I have an incredible attitude. I know I can do it, get past the negatives, focus everything I do on the most positive outcome, and do it."

May 18

"If I had one day, one time, one moment, to live up to my best, take action, get things done, move forward and excel, I would do it. And as soon as I think the thought, I know the truth: Today is the day, this is the time, and right now is the moment."

Self-Talk Tip #19

Your Brain Can *"Delete"* Old Mental Programs You No Longer Want!

Does your brain, like a computer, have a delete button? Researchers have learned that in your brain, when you stop using an old program, you stop sending nutrition to that program's neural networks; you stop *feeding* it, and in time your brain will delete it.

Neuroscientists call this "pruning." Like the gardener who cuts out, or prunes, old rose branches to make way for new growth and more beautiful roses, the brain will get rid of pathways you're no longer using to make way for new pathways to form.

If you'd like to prune out old programs you no longer want, the best way we've found to deal with them is to replace them with new programs—new self-talk—which, with enough repetition, will eventually become the stronger programs and take over. When you stop using the old programs, they will lose their nutrition, and in time, your brain will prune them out. And beautiful new roses will grow.

May 19

"Each new day is a chance for me to live up to my dreams. What l want to do, l can do. What l want to achieve, l can achieve. And who l want to become, l can become. l choose to dream my dreams, set my goals, work hard, and make my dreams come true. That's what l choose to do, with each new day."

May 20

"I know that the secret to unlocking the doorway to my most positive future is my own self-talk and every thought I think each day. So I make sure that the messages I give to myself are filled with self-belief, self confidence, determination to succeed, and an absolute certainty that the best is yet to come."

May 21

"There is nothing that is possible, that I cannot accomplish when I put my mind to it, and decide to do it. I am living a life of unlimited possibilities. And all I have to do is decide what I want to achieve, put myself into action, take the first step, then keep moving, and refuse to give up! That's how dreams come true."

May 22

"It is my right to raise myself up, to get better, and to improve myself in every way I can. People who refuse to grow do little for themselves, and less for the world around them. People who improve their lives in positive ways make the world better for everyone."

May 23

"I can't wait to go for it. Just imagine what I can do. My plans, my goals, my future, anything I choose— creating my freedom, sharing with others, working hard, getting things done, and feeling good about myself. I can't wait to make things happen. So today, I'm not waiting. Today I'm going for it!"

May 24

"I practice seeing myself as I most want to be. I see myself doing what I truly want to do. I see myself being healthy and in great shape. I see myself accomplishing great things. I see myself being at peace and happy with my life. The more I see myself that way, the more I create what I see."

Self-Talk Tip #20
Your Self-Talk Today Is Creating the Person You're Going to Become Tomorrow

Imagine what would happen if the way you talked to yourself today would create the person you'd meet in the mirror tomorrow. That's exactly what's happening, but many people aren't aware of it. You're wiring who you're going to be, in the future, into your brain right now.

Once you know this, you can change or improve who you'd like to become, and you can start the process by the thoughts you think.

Are you as happy as you'd like to be? Would you like to be smarter? Do you want to do better in your relationships? How about your job; are you the best you can be at what you do? What about your talents and skills? Are you living up to what you could have been, or have old programs convinced you you're not as good as you'd like to be? None of those things are accidents. They're the result of your programs. And programs can be changed.

The self-talk you practice today will create the 'you' you're going to become tomorrow. That means that most of life really isn't the result of blind luck or fate. It's up to the programs you create. And those programs are entirely up to you.

May 25

"I dream 'day dreams' that open my world to the wonderful possibilities that are in front of me. Instead of worrying about my future and what I will do with it, I dream of it, I create it, and I make it happen."

May 26

"I see myself and my journey in the most positive possible way. I am learning, I am growing, and I am finding and living my reason for being."

May 27

"I was born with unlimited potential, so I choose to learn and continue to grow. I choose to live up to my unlimited promise. I choose to become the me I was intended to be."

May 28

"My life is good. The moment I think about it, I realize how true that is. I'm here, I'm alive, and I have so many wonderful chances to live up to best. Every day I'm here is a blessing and an opportunity. Once again, today, my whole life is in front of me, and I know that my life is good."

May 29

"My attitude is always up to me. Whenever I feel down, I choose to change my attitude and get myself feeling up again. No matter what's happening in my life, I choose to think up, be positive, feel confident, and believe in the bright promise of my future. When I choose to have a winning attitude, my whole world changes for the better."

May 30

"I choose not to worry, or fear anything that tomorrow brings. I am strong, I am capable, and I am confident in my ability to anticipate, make plans, take the right action, and deal with anything that comes my way. I choose to believe in the best, and when I do, the best is what I get."

May 31

"On one hand I have humility. On the other I have strength and confidence. On one hand I pray that my life will work out right. On the other hand I know it's up to me."

Author's Notes:
The Three Questions

When I was quite young, in my early teens, I conceived the notion that in order to find my calling in life I would have to answer three important questions. I wrote out the three questions, and thought about them a lot. It would take time before I found the answers to each of them, but I finally did. Here are the three questions I asked:

- The first question was, ***"What?"*** If I was going to do something of value, something that would be the most important thing in my life, what would that be? • The second question was ***"How?"*** Only after I had answered the first question could I begin to find the answer to the question of how I would accomplish my goal, and what preparation I would need. • The third question was, ***"When?"*** If everything has its time, I wanted to be sure that my *What* and *How* were brought to life in the right time.

Finding the answer to each of the three questions took several years, but it was my first real quest, and I felt an important one, so I stayed with it. I finally found my answers and I followed them; I'm following them still. But the important thing about the three questions was that *asking* them changed my life, and played a role in directing almost everything I would ever do. Those three questions were my way of finding my purpose. Perhaps those same three questions will help you find yours.

— S.H.

June 1

"I never let myself overstress or get upset with the unimportant things in life. I take life seriously, but never more seriously than it deserves to be taken. I stay practical, always keep my balance, make sure my vision of tomorrow is clear and strong, and let the small things pass."

June 2

"Finding my purpose is not an accident; it is the result of my willingness to search, and my determination to find it."

June 3

"I know that I may have many purposes, big and small, many chances to find them, and endless opportunities to bring them to life. The more I search, the more I find."

June 4

"Today I choose to think about what I would like my purpose to be. So I ask myself the question, "If my purpose could be anything, what would I like it to be?" The more I ask the question, the more clearly I hear the answer."

June 5

"By keeping myself fit, my mind alert, and my attitude positive, I am ready to live up to the purpose I am attracting in my life."

June 6

"The most important step in finding my purpose is making the choice to search for it."

Self-Talk Tip #21
A Helpful History of Self-Talk

The idea of changing our lives by changing our self-talk is very old. The Bible suggested the idea of self-talk in Proverbs 23:7, *"As a man thinketh in his heart, so is he."* Romans 12:2 said it even more directly: *" . . . be transformed by the renewing of your mind."* But the idea of using positive self-talk techniques for consciously reprogramming our minds would wait more than two thousand years before it would be accepted as scientific fact.

In the mid 1950s, following the 1920s-era writings of French pharmacologist Emile Coué, pioneering self-help authors such as Napolean Hill, Dr. Norman Vincent Peale, Dr. Maxwell Maltz and others, began to bring the concepts of positive thinking and conscious "autosuggestion" to the attention of self-help followers.

It was not, however, until the 1980's that self-talk, as it is used today, began to be generally understood. When researchers, using computer imaging technology, were finally able to see into the living brain, their research showed that because of the brain's ability to rewire itself (neuroplasticity), *self-talk*, practiced in the right way, could actually restructure the individual's brain with new neural networks.

Neuroscientists and behavioral researchers found that new input to the brain, such as specially-worded self-talk, could rewire and change not only the brain's physical structure, but also the individual's attitudes, actions, and results as well. We had discovered that our *thoughts* physically rewire our brains—and the science of self-talk was born.

June 7

"I have purpose, great value, and an important reason for being. I'm not here to wander without direction; I'm here to get something done."

June 8

"I practice letting go. When it's time to move on or move past something in my life that is not part of my future, I think it through, am always mindful of the consequences of what I do next, and if it's right to let it go, I let it go."

June 9

"The more I focus on finding my reason for being, the more positive possibilities come into my life. So I keep myself focused, alert, aware, and ready."

June 10

"I choose to never compare my own accomplishments to the achievements of others. I choose, instead, to spend my time improving myself and finding ways I can do better, not so that I can rise above someone else, but so I can learn to rise above myself."

June 11

"I make every morning important. When I awake I always greet the day with gratitude for my life and appreciation for being here, this one day. Then I think about what I can do today to express my life in the most positive, helpful way, and make the world a better place because I am here, and get to live my life, this one day."

June 12

"I think for myself. I may listen to others, and measure what they say, but I determine for myself the truths of my life. Instead of following blindly, I think for myself. Instead of accepting what everyone else thinks or does, I think for myself. And when, each day, I take the next step into my future, I think for myself."

Self-Talk Tip #22

Is Your Brain Wired to *Succeed*?

What really makes the difference in our lives? Why are some people successful, and other people are not?

Research tells us that our brains become wired for success or failure. As we grew, each of us got programs from the world around us, and many of those programs became 'permanently' wired into our brains. Those programs (neural networks in our brain) determine every thought we think and every action we take—which leads, inevitably, to success or failure in anything we do.

Since we were born, each of our brains has been recording, storing, and wiring in programs we received from parents, teachers, friends, and the world around us. If we were fortunate, and our brains got wired with enough programs that are positive and healthy, we live our lives in a positive, healthy, successful way. If, on the other hand, we got too many of the wrong kind of programs, we end up struggling—or failing—because of the programs we got. (No one *intended* to wire us to fail, of course.)

If we receive too many of the wrong kinds of programs, we end up living with them and wishing things could be better—or we *change* them.

Fortunately, our brains were designed to help us get rid of programs we don't want. That's why we practice positive self-talk—so we can change our programs. And this time we're going to get them *right*.

June 13

"I dream big, but I'm also very practical. I set specific goals, I put my plans in writing, and I take each action step I need to take. I dream great dreams, but I also take every step I need to take to turn my dreams into reality."

June 14

"The true purpose of my life is bigger than any day, any problem, any challenge, any misstep, any setback, or anything that could cause me to lose sight of why I am here."

June 15

"Problems don't bother me. Difficulties never stop me. Life and it's demands can't get me off course. I have a purpose, and as long as I keep that in mind, *nothing* stops me."

June 16

"There are so many people I can help. There are so many things I can do. There is so much I have to offer. To get started, all I have to do is choose my path and follow it."

June 17

"I have a job to do. An important, special, and valuable job that only I can do. That's why I'm here. That's what I came here to do."

June 18

"I listen to my wishes and my dreams. They tell me how I would like things to be, what I would like to do, and what I would like to make of this amazing life I have been given."

Self-Talk Tip #23
Why Do People Who Practice Positive Self-Talk Do *Better?*

Over all, people who think in a positive, optimistic way, and who actively practice using positive self-talk, tend to do better in dealing with problems than people who are negative. Why is that?

The answer is based on neuroscience. Thinking negatively shuts down the creative, open-minded qualities of the brain. Positive "self-talkers" are open to more alternatives, so they have more choices when it comes to solving problems and dealing with life. They literally see more solutions than people whose horizons are limited by negative thinking.

Neurologically speaking, positive self-talk 'wires in' the idea of giving yourself more choices, and being willing to see the possibility of succeeding. While negative self-talk convinces you to stop trying, practicing positive self-talk keeps you looking for a more successful outcome, until the right solution can be found.

June 19

"I slow life down by controlling the thoughts I think and the focus of my mind. I never allow the meaningless, high-speed chaos of the world around me to pull me into its race to nowhere. I stand quietly, outside of the rush, away from the noise, calmly focused on a precious moment in a beautiful day."

June 20

"I listen to the quiet voice within me that is wise, caring, understanding, and always there when I choose to listen. I go to a quiet place in my mind, ask my question in clear, simple words, and wait for an answer. When I ask my question, wait with patience, and listen carefully, the answer always comes"

June 21

"I know that the most important words I ever say, are the words I say to myself. So I make sure I give myself the right dreams, the right goals, the right direction, the right attitude, the right strength, and the thankfulness for what I achieve."

June 22

"Each day my self-talk wires my brain with a picture of the person I will become tomorrow. If I am 'down' on me, my brain will believe it, wire it in, and pull me down. If I am 'up' on me, my brain will be wired to help me succeed. The truth is, my tomorrow is up to me."

June 23

"I am a person of quality. I speak clearly, tell the truth, choose to be strong, and am a person of direction and goals. I am honest with myself and others, I have both dreams of unlimited potential and the humility to appreciate every blessing that comes to my life."

June 24

"Because I have purpose, I bring happiness into my life every day. I am on my journey, and I look forward with joy and enthusiasm to every step I take along the way."

Self-Talk Tip #24
Super-Charging Your Self-Talk

Years ago, when self-talk was first introduced, it became immediately apparent that positive self-talk could be super-charged by listening to it.

Early self-talk was first recorded on cassette tapes, and later on CDs. Today, people who want to take self-talk to the next level listen to digital self-talk programs on their tablets and smartphones.

The reason listening to self-talk helps is because of the role of *repetition* in rewiring the brain. The most important rule of neuroplasticity for rewiring the brain is repetition. (We still remember the words to songs we heard when we were kids, when all we did was hear them played in the background. We learn new self-talk in the same way.)

Recorded self-talk goes into depth to get to the heart of issues like purpose, goals, self-esteem, relationships, stress, work, finances, etc. It rewires a broad group of programs in the brain that work together to create new attitudes and beliefs about the subject the listener is focusing on.

This kind of super-charged self-talk is listened to daily, and it is clearly the daily repetition that does the trick; hearing self-talk repeated in this way forms new neural pathways that are imprinted in the brain. People listen while they're getting ready in the morning, or while they're driving in the car, or when they're at the office or around the house, or when they're going to sleep at night.

You can listen to self-talk programs that are certified by the Self-Talk Institute at SelfTalkPlus.com.

June 25

"I stand up for my goals. I consider the thoughts of others whose input is positive and supportive, but the choice of my path in life is up to me."

June 26

"I watch my old programs playing out in my mind, and I realize why I have had to work so hard in my life. Within my old programs I see my own resistance to making changes in my life, my own unnecessary fears about my ability to survive and do well, and old programs that doubt the successes of my own future. Those are all old, negative and unnecessary programs, and I choose to get rid of them. I no longer need them, and I will do much better without them."

June 27

"I choose to listen to the earliest dreams of my childhood, and the unlimited possibilities for the life that I saw in my youth. So I stop now, see clearly the person I wanted to be, and ask myself the question: *Have I lived my dream? And if I haven't, could I still?*"

June 28

"Today is an incredible day! I am so blessed to be able to live my life with a purpose that adds value to everything I do."

June 29

"When I think about quitting, or giving up on something important to me, and I know I should keep going, I take time to get my thinking right. I remember my purpose, I regain my focus, I choose to make things work, and I come back stronger than ever."

June 30

"Living up to my purpose may require a lot from me, but I'm up to it. Whatever I need, I will have. Whatever I require, I will be given."

Author's Notes:
Changing Your Direction

What if you find your purpose, dedicate your choices to making that purpose a driving force in your life, and then something changes, and your 'lifelong purpose' doesn't feel like your lifelong purpose anymore? In it's positive form, that's called 'growth.'

There is no universal truth that dictates we are limited to just one important purpose, and to that purpose only. (One very wise teacher of mine maintained that we all have eight or more of them.) Whatever the number, it's clear that if the reason you're here is to learn, grow, and get better, then along with each important step in your growth you could expect *change*, and along with that change could come a change in purpose—bringing you to the next step 'up' in your direction in life. It is as though each time you've completed your purpose, you're given a larger key which opens a more beautiful door to an even greater purpose, waiting for you to discover it.

We are living in a world of virtually unlimited possibilities. There is more we *could* do than we can even imagine. So the opportunity to find and express more than one purpose is an incredible blessing— like being able to live more than one lifetime. (Which answers the question about finding more than one purpose in your life.) Finding first one purpose, and then others, is not the exception. It's the natural order of things.

– S.H.

July 1

"Today I'm going for it! I know my goal, I know what I want to do, and I know that all I have to do is do it. So I choose to take control of my day, stop the excuses, put myself into motion, take action, put all of my energy into making it work, and refuse to stop until I reach the goal."

July 2

"I give myself permission to dream incredible dreams of my purpose and my future. I know that dreams *can* come true, and that I will live the best of my dreams."

July 3

"I make the time to spend my time with people who are upbeat, positive, and going for it! The more I surround myself with people who succeed, the more positive I am, the more I learn, the better I do, and the more successful I become!"

July 4

"I never wait for someone else to lift me up, set my course, or get me moving. I know that my success is up to me. What I believe is what I achieve. And every day I choose to be mindful of my purpose, believe in the best and create my success."

July 5

"To find my purpose, I listen. I listen to my thoughts, I listen to my dreams, and I listen to the guiding voice within me."

July 6

"It's not 'luck' that makes my life work; it's how I look at it. I choose to see the bright, find the good, believe in a positive outcome, and always have faith that I will overcome the challenges and succeed. And because that's how I choose to look at my life every day, time after time, I win!"

Self-Talk Tip #25
From *Self-Talk* to *Success* in 5 Steps

One of the subjects the book *What to Say When You Talk to Your Self* discusses in detail is the process by which changing your self-talk leads to actual changes that take place in your real life. Here it is in a nutshell:

1. When you change your self-talk, you change what you **believe** about yourself.
2. When you change what you believe about yourself, you change your **attitude**.
3. When you change your attitude, you change your **feelings**.
4. When you change your feelings, you change your **actions**.
5. When you change your actions, you change your **results**.

To test this for yourself, think of something in your life (or in yourself) you'd like to improve. Then focus on that area of your self-talk for two or three weeks. When it comes to that subject, give it your full attention, and completely change *all* of your self-talk about that subject—to the positive.

When you do that, and stay with it, you will change your belief, your attitude, your feelings, your actions, and your results.

July 7

"Today I choose to focus on my goals, get a clear picture of what I need to do next, make the decision to take action, get my attitude in shape, put myself into motion, and make today a get-it-done day!"

July 8

"I am always mindful of being mindful. I am consciously aware of being aware. Because I'm mindful, I listen to what I say, and I also listen carefully to my thoughts. Because I'm mindful, I'm in control of what I think, what I say, and how I feel."

July 9

"I choose to see my own future as a bright, positive, healthy, exciting place to be. That's the future I choose to live. And today and every day, in everything I do, that's the future I choose to create."

July 10

"When it comes to my attitude, I'm up! When it comes to my goal, I'm going for it! When it comes to staying with it, I'm there! And when it comes to making my day an incredible day, I'm on it, I've got it, and I'm making it happen!"

July 11

"I know that one reason I am here is to live up to my best. Instead of just getting by, I make sure that I create the highest quality in my life."

July 12

"If I could do anything that I wanted to do that is possible and doable, what would it be? Without the limitations of self-doubt or disbelief, what could I accomplish?"

Self-Talk Tip #26

'Tying a String Around Your Finger' to Keep You Mindful of Your Purpose

Before the days of smartphones and smart watches, people sometimes tied a string around their finger to remind them of something important they wanted to remember during the day. Reading positive self-talk messages daily is a similar kind of reminder, and it is especially helpful when it comes to being mindful of your purpose—every day.

Each self-talk message you read each day not only gives you a positive perspective on the day, it also reminds you that every thought you think that day is important. The more days you focus on the idea *that your thoughts wire and change your brain*, the more mindful and aware of your thoughts you'll become. And the more mindful you are, the more you take control of your thoughts, your life, your direction, and your destiny. When it comes to living your purpose in life, that makes a small daily reminder a very big thing.

July 13

"Of all the people who help me, influence me, or guide me in any way, the one person who has the most control over my thoughts, my actions, and the direction of my life is the person I spend the most time with each day. The one person who holds the key to who I am and who I will be, is me."

July 14

"To find my purpose, I know I have to accept the truth that my potential is unlimited. Starting right now, I accept my unlimited potential."

July 15

"I know that the only real limitations I place on my potential, are the limitations I place on myself. When it comes to finding my purpose, I get rid of any imagined limitations I might have had."

July 16

"I have been given the incredible gift of being me.
So I choose to live up to the promise only I can fulfill.
I have so much to discover, and so much to live; so
much to offer, and so much to give. And every day
I choose to live up to my best, and to become the
me I was created to be."

July 17

"I do my best when I feel good about myself, and how I feel
about myself is always up to me. So right now I take a good
look at the real me, and choose to like who I see. I can always
get better, but I like who I am and I'm glad to be me."

July 18

"I am a person of exceptional quality. I have skills,
talents, abilities, and potentials that make me special in
so many ways. That is the real me as I was intended to
be. How do I know? That's the way God made me in
the first place, and God makes winners, not mistakes."

Self-Talk Tip #27
How Self-Talk Works

Your brain needs a lot of healthy programs in order for you to succeed or do well in life. Self-talk is a way for you to get positive new programs wired into your brain. It's based on neuroscience—on how the brain works—but it isn't hard to understand:

Your brain records every message you give it. The part of the brain that records those messages doesn't know the difference between something that is *true,* and something that is *false.* Positive or negative, bad or good, your brain just records it, and then acts on it. Any message you send to your brain *repeatedly* (by reading, speaking, or listening) gets wired in, and your brain acts on it as though it's *true*—whether or not it was true to begin with.

Giving your brain the right self-talk messages physically wires your brain with positive, new neural pathways that in time become the new you —but with better programs. Your day-to-day success is based on the number of positive neural pathways that get wired in.

The more you practice using the right self-talk, the more healthy, new neural pathways you wire into your brain.

July 19

"Where do I find my greatest happiness and joy day after day? I find the best of me in being the real me, and living for the reason I am here."

July 20

"I don't mind it when others question my goals or think I can't reach them. I know that real winners win by following their greatest dreams, rather than listening to the negative opinions of others. So I don't give up, and I don't give in. And because I keep believing in myself, I win!"

July 21

"I know that having a life-long goal gives foundation to my life and substance to every other goal I set. Searching for my primary goal, and finding it, affects everything I do in a positive way."

July 22

"I can't wait to greet the day each morning. I have so many goals, dreams, and possibilities in front of me, and I choose to make my dreams come true. So every day I wake up, think up, get up, and go for it!"

July 23

"I refuse to walk aimlessly on the road of 'average.' I will not live without purpose, without direction, and without a powerful goal to guide me. But I know that I *do* have a purpose, and living for that purpose is my #1 goal."

July 24

"I alone choose every thought I think. I alone am responsible for the direction of my day. I may be surrounded by the love, help, and support of others. But I alone must choose my path, and I alone will find my way."

Self-Talk Tip #28

Everyone Has a Purpose

There is no one who does not have a purpose. You have a purpose (probably several of them) and everyone you'll ever meet has a purpose, including those who never think about it or have no idea what their purpose might be.

For some it may be raising a family and giving their children an exceptional head-start in life. For others it may be creating beauty and depth of feeling through art, or music. Purpose for some may be excelling in their work or career, while for others it may be learning or teaching. Still others find their purpose in helping others, or healing, or inspiring others.

One of the secrets to living a fulfilling life is in discovering your purpose, whatever it may be. So taking the time to discover it becomes very important. It is a process that best begins with the assumption that your purpose is already there, within you, waiting to be found.

This is why you'll find self-talk passages in these pages that let you know your purpose is waiting for you, as though a higher part of you has already chosen it and is encouraging you to find it and live it.

July 25

"I refuse to worry, or let the challenges of the moment, or the problems of the day get me down. I'm here, I'm alive, I'm alert, I'm awake, and aware, and I'm ready to make today a successful day in every way!"

July 26

"I choose to live my life by choice, not by chance. My success each day, each hour and each moment, is not up to luck or fortune; it is up to the choices I make. And because I choose success, I choose to make good choices."

July 27

"Changing my life for the better, by thinking right, thinking up, and choosing to succeed, always works best with practice. So I practice looking at life in the most positive possible way, every day. And the more I practice, the better I get."

July 28

"A person without purpose is a person who runs the race without a goal. I choose to live up to the purpose of my highest calling, and the steps I take, I take for a reason."

July 29

"Today is incredibly important! What I do with this one day, *counts*. Fulfilling my life's purpose may be essential to my happiness and well-being, but living today in a positive way, is just as important."

July 30

"When it comes to 'goals of self,' and my purpose in life, I do my best to ignore the rules of 'fitting in,' or being 'average.' I didn't come here to just 'get by.' I came here to make a difference."

July 31

"I know that the key to finding my purpose is the amount of attention I give it. My reason for being is already within me, and the closer I look, the clearer it becomes."

Author's Notes:
Are You Called to the Quest?

People who have the greatest sense of purpose seem to be those who feel they are 'called' to the quest. They express an 'inner knowing' that they have come here for an important reason, and finding that reason and fulfilling it creates their direction in life. So many people feel this sense of being *called*, that it's clearly more than a quirk of human nature; it's built into our spiritual consciousness, and the more we listen for it, the more we hear its message.

One of the reasons to actively search for our purpose is that it is in that search that we take the time to stop and listen for the calling. When you ask what you are sent here to do, and keep asking, in time you hear the answer. You can listen in prayer, in meditation, in introspection and self-discovery. Just keep asking, and keep listening.

It's my personal observation that *everyone* is called. Everyone has a purpose. But our culture programs us with so many distractions that many people never recognize that life consists of more than fitting in with 'average,' working, retiring, and dying. They never realize that life could be so much more; that there is a reason and a purpose for being here in the first place. They don't know there is a calling—and that by listening for that calling, their lives could change forever, in incredibly wonderful and fulfilling ways.

– S.H.

August 1

"If I ever have trouble identifying my purpose, I know what to do: I change my perspective, look in new places, explore new ideas, and search for new options. The more I'm open to new ideas, the more I find."

August 2

"Why do I wait for something better? Why would I put off my future, when I can start right now? Today I choose to take control of my life, decide what I want to do next, set my goals, put myself into action, and take a clear, positive step *up* into my own, unlimited future."

August 3

"Every day I look forward to the quest. The joy of searching for my purpose is equal to the joy of finding it."

August 4

"Searching for my purpose in life is a purpose in itself. In my search I learn more about who I am, what's important to me, and what I would most like to do to with the gifts my life has given me."

August 5

"I have patience. I understand that some things take time. When I need to get something done, I do it, but when I have to wait for time to run its course, I consciously take the time to understand, wait with an attitude of calm and quiet, and appreciate the opportunity to watch my world work."

August 6

"When I'm in alignment with my true purpose in life, other things fall into place, I overcome obstacles more easily, I reach more of my goals, and every day has more meaning."

Self-Talk Tip #29

Clearing Out Your 'Mental Apartment'

Imagine that you live in a "mental apartment." You've had the same old furniture for years. (The "furniture" is your old mental programs.) You got your hand-me-down furniture—your old way of thinking—from your family, parents, teachers, friends, and all of your past. It's old furniture. It's tattered and worn, but you're used to it, and it's all you know—it's your old way of thinking.

Now let's say you want to clear out your mental apartment, so you decide to get rid of all of your old mental furniture by getting rid of all of your old negative mental programs. So you take all of that old furniture out and store it out of sight in your garage.

The next morning you wake up to a beautifully empty mental apartment. No old negative furniture. No old easy chair of negative opinions. No old desk with drawers full of bad attitudes. No old television set spewing out negative programs. Your mental apartment is completely empty, and you realize you have nowhere to sit or do anything.

(Continued)

So what do you do next? After a while you go out to the garage and start bringing the *old* furniture back in! First you bring back in that old easy chair of negative opinions—the one you were going to get rid of. And then, later the same day, you bring in the old desk. That night, you bring back in the old television set. Finally, after just a day or two, your entire mental apartment is filled back up with the same old, tattered, *negative* furniture that you were used to living with. Why did you bring it all back in? *Because you didn't have any new furniture to replace it with.*

If you want to get rid of the old negative furniture in your life, you have to replace it with something better. You have to get new positive "furniture"—new programs—or your *old* programs will come back in!

The new furniture is your new self-talk. Positive self-talk replaces the old negative furniture in your mental apartment with new, positive programs. When you learn the new self-talk, you change the furniture in your mental apartment for good. And that's the beginning of changing your life.

From *What to Say When You Talk to Your Self* by Shad Helmstetter, Ph.D.

August 7

"I refuse to ever let unnecessary worry or fear rule my life. I'm strong, I'll get through it, I'll get past it, and I'll be better because of it. Any time I feel worries or fears tugging at my mind, I immediately give myself the self-talk that says, 'I'm up to this, I can do this, I'm strong, I'm capable, I'm bigger than the problem, and this too shall pass.'"

August 8

"When it comes to my own path in life, I pay no attention to any doubts or disbelief from others. I stay focused on my goals, stay on course, and keep moving forward."

August 9

"I don't just stop and smell the roses. Every day, day after day, I stop and appreciate my life. I always remember that every day I live is a day filled with countless blessings, endless hope, and unlimited promise. Just to be here and to be me is an incredible blessing, and I know it and I show it every day."

August 10

"I am more than I could ever have imagined. I am responsible, and I always take care of my work and the day-to-day obligations of my life. But there is more to me than my work, or the daily details of my life. My possibilities are endless, my future is unlimited, and I always take the time to remember that I was also designed to soar with the eagles."

August 11

"Money may be essential, and having enough is important. But wealth, to me, is more than dollars and material possessions. I choose to measure my life not by how much I can possess, but by who I am as a person, what I'm doing with my gifts, and how much I'm helping others."

August 12

"I will never stop seeking and learning. I choose to listen, study, find new interests, always be curious, keep an open mind, correct myself, learn new things, keep on growing, and never stop. As long as I am here, I will not only excel, I will truly live."

Self-Talk Tip #30
Extra Help for Practicing Self-Talk

When you're practicing positive self-talk, here's something that will help.

One of the benefits of reading positive self-talk every day is that it gives you a pattern to follow—a style of self-talk you can adapt and apply to your everyday life. Good self-talk is a habit that will come with practice, and paying close attention to the self-talk messages you're reading each day will help.

Each time an opportunity comes up—and there will be many of them—practice rephrasing your thoughts, and what you say out loud to others, with the same kinds of word and phrases you read here. Every situation is different, but with practice you'll find that you're not only *talking* more positively in general, you'll also find yourself *thinking* that way, even when you're not focused on being positive.

Self-talk phrases like *"I choose to make today an incredible day,"* or *"I'm on top, in tune, in touch, and going for it,"* become more than words on a page; they become a way to pattern the rest of your thoughts throughout the day.

The goal, as a positive self-talker, is to be mindful of all of your thoughts, and consciously aware of the importance of your self-talk. The self-talk passages you read here can inspire a lot of good ideas, and, when you're getting started, they'll give you a helpful pattern to follow.

August 13

"I choose to practice the incredible art and skill of day dreaming. I get rid of the limits; go beyond the boundaries; and in my mind, fly to the farthest reaches of my imagination. When I'm dreaming of the endless universe of potential that surrounds me, I am wiring my brain to take me there."

August 14

"I choose to be happy. I know that being happy, day by day, is a choice. And because happiness is also physically healthy, attitude-adjusting, mood-elevating, emotionally stabilizing, success-generating, immediately uplifting, day-changing, and contagious, I choose to be happy."

August 15

"I refuse to let set-backs or disappointments get me down. That's life, and life is exactly as good as I choose to make it. So I choose to see life in the most positive, optimistic way. I always deal with the challenges of today, but I never forget the unlimited possibilities of tomorrow."

August 16

"I choose to live a life that adds to the lives of others. I believe in, care about, uplift, support, and encourage others. Living in service to the lives of others adds value, purpose, and meaning to my life every day."

August 17

"I avoid spending time with people who are negative, cannot see my vision, or do not believe in the value of purpose. What they do is up to them, but I choose to never let their lack of belief diminish mine."

August 18

"I spend no time doing things that only drain my resources and energy, and offer little or no value in return. I stay focused on my purpose, and choose to do those things that build my vitality and my output in every healthy way."

Self-Talk Tip #31
Three Steps to Changing
Your Programs

Your brain is built to constantly wire and rewire itself with new information; it is designed to change its programs if you tell it what to do. There are three steps you can take that will help you do that.

Step 1 – *Monitor.* Monitor means to listen to everything you say when you're talking to someone *else*, everything you say when you're talking to *yourself*, and even the thoughts you *think*. Consciously listen to everything you say or think.

Step 2 – *Edit.* You have the ability to edit and change anything you are about to say, or anything you're about to think. If what you were going to say or think next is actually negative self-talk, *don't say it. Don't think it.* Change it. Turn it around. Get it right. Turn it into a positive.

Step 3 – *Listen.* The best way to change old programs rapidly is by listening to new self-talk. It was by hearing the messages that were spoken to us originally that we received most of our old programming; it is by hearing the *right* self-talk repeated that those old programs are most easily changed.

People now listen to recorded self-talk sessions that are streamed to their tablets or smartphones. When you listen in this way, it's like learning a new language—by listening to it repeatedly until it gets wired in.

You can experience listening to self-talk programs on your smartphone or listening device at SelfTalkPlus.com.

August 19

"My purpose of my life is greater than any doubts or limited thoughts I might have had. My horizons reach farther and my potential is greater than I can possibly imagine."

August 20

"Today is a great day! Not only do I know I have purpose, but I also know that finding it is an important part of my journey. And today I get to be on my journey."

August 21

"The more I look for my purpose and meaning, the more of it I find. When it comes to finding purpose in my life, the most important step is to look for it."

August 22

"I practice having a happy, positive mind. The more optimistic I am, the more I train and prepare my brain for success. The more positive I see my life, the more opportunities come my way, the more doors are open to me, the more I grow, and the more peace of mind and happiness I create."

August 23

"It is often the smallest things in life that have the greatest value. My purpose, big or small, is important."

August 24

"I refuse to measure my life by comparing myself to anyone else. I am living my life for my reasons, my purpose, and my destiny, not theirs. My goal is not to be as good as someone else; my goal is to be as good as I was created to be."

Self-Talk Tip #32
The Importance of *Today*

It can take time to find the great purpose in life that's perfect for you. But what do you do to live up to your highest potential while you wait for your purpose to be revealed to you? Does not quite knowing your purpose mean you have to drift without direction? Not at all. In fact, the time you spend while you're searching and waiting to discover your purpose can give you practice in one of the most important lessons you can ever learn: the importance of living *today*.

You don't have to be fulfilling your highest calling at this moment to make today, right now, a time of exceptional quality, aliveness, and awareness of the value of 'now.' The *reason* we may have to wait to find our purpose, is to give us time to prepare for it. It's a time to align our thoughts to our higher consciousness, a spiritual boot camp in which we prepare to live up to the destiny we have chosen.

Each day, as you follow your quest and search for your reason for being, see the day as a wonderful opportunity to touch the *now*, feel it, taste it, savor it, experience it and learn everything you can from living it. The *now* is your opportunity to be completely alive today, while you prepare for the exciting world of your tomorrow.

August 25

"I listen to my regular, everyday voice. But I also listen carefully to the voice that is the higher, wiser part of me. To hear my wiser, inner voice, I make sure that I take the time, find the quiet, go within, be patient, and listen carefully. And the more I listen, the better my life works."

August 26

"The lives of others tell us which of them live for a greater purpose and which do not. The happiest, most productive people have found theirs, and it is my choice to find mine."

August 27

"I choose to be alive, alert, and aware. I am endlessly curious, interested in new things, always ready to learn, and getting smarter every day. I'm not just hoping or wishing I could improve who I am. I'm practicing personal growth every day, and it's working."

August 28

"I know that the path I choose to take in life is mine to find and mine to follow. I may have guidance and support along the way, and some of my steps may ask for the help and belief of others, but the path I follow is mine to choose and up to me."

August 29

"I am an active thinker, and never a lazy thinker. Instead of letting my mind drift aimlessly from thought to thought, I practice being consciously aware of every thought I think. With practice, I not only become more mindful of my own thoughts, I choose thoughts that are clear, lead me forward, and improve my life."

August 30

"When it comes to my purpose, and what it may be, I am never afraid to reach high, expect the best, and live up to my greatest calling."

August 31

"If I ever doubt my purpose, or if I'm not certain what my purpose may be, I pay attention, gather information, write an actual list of possibilities, and look for ideas that speak to me in the deepest possible way."

Author's Notes:
Finding the Greatest Purpose in the Smallest Things

Many people struggle with finding their purpose because they believe that for someone to have a great purpose, they have to do great things. But they're not going to climb Mt. Everest, they're not going to inspire a nation or find the cure for a disease. So they feel that great purpose is for others, but not for themselves.

The truth is, great purpose is for everyone. (As it says in Matthew 25:40 *"Whatever you did for one of the least of these brothers and sisters of mine, you did for me."*) The true quality of the individual isn't measured by the size of the achievement, but rather by the intent and growth of the individual. It can be argued that a person's sole reason for living their life is to grow and improve themselves to their highest degree, and do so while creating the highest good for others. That growth could be attained for one person by climbing mountains, and for another person by tending roses.

When you search for your purpose, do your best to ignore the false importance our culture places on the temporary forms of celebrity, wealth or riches so often presented as 'success.' It may well be the least celebrated, or the smallest things in life, that prove to be your highest purpose.

– S.H.

143

September 1

"When it comes to creating my best possible future, I have patience. I am willing to work for, and wait for, the positive results of my efforts to come into my life. I think ahead, plan ahead, and stay with it. And I'm willing to be patient and wait for the results."

September 2

"When someone says "I cannot," I answer "Why not?" When someone says "It's impossible," I answer that nothing is any more impossible than I believe it to be. And today, with my incredible attitude and positive self-talk working for me, anything good is possible."

September 3

"There is nothing that can stop me or hold me back from my own success and my unlimited future. When it comes to my future, what counts most is me, and the next choice I make."

September 4

"My age, right now, or how much time has gone by in my life, does not limit me from fulfilling my purpose. Every day I have spent up to now has been in preparation for the wonderful opportunities to come."

September 5

"I refuse to ever feel held back or defeated by the challenges or the problems of the life I'm living today. I choose to follow my purpose, and it is my purpose, not the problems, that direct my choices, my path, and my future."

September 6

"If I had just one life to live, and I could do anything I wanted, what would I do? This *is* my life, I *can* do what I choose, and I get to decide what I do."

Self-Talk Tip #33

What Stops Us From Being That Amazing Person We Dreamed About Becoming?

When they're young, most people dream about doing something special with their lives. A lot of those early dreams *could* be reached, but they're not. What goes wrong?

Research tells us that most of our success is the result of the way our brains get "wired." Our beliefs about ourselves are the result of the wiring we get from others, and eventually from our own self-talk.

When we're young, and believe anything is possible, our brain hasn't yet been wired with what we *cannot* do. It just accepts us as being unlimited, with little or no disbelief to get in the way of our dreams.

But all too soon we're told—by people around us—what *won't* work and what we *can't* do, and our brain starts to wire those messages in as though they're *true*—even if they weren't really true when we first heard them. In time, many of those disbelieving messages become permanently wired into our once unlimited brains. And we replace our dreams with limitations. We could have done almost anything, but we got wired to do something less.

Thanks to positive self-talk we can change that. Because we can *change* our programs, and rewire our brains with the right self-talk, we can bring some of those old dreams back to life—or create new dreams that are just as good. And this time we won't let anyone take them away.

September 7

"I choose to create abundance in my life. Always healthy, always good, always more than I need, and always enough to share with others. With my attitude, the choices I make, and the actions I take, I create abundance in my life."

September 8

"When I see it in the right light, life is wonderful and beautiful. Today especially. That's what I choose. That's how I choose to see my day."

September 9

"What am I doing today to make the world a better place? Whether it's a big step or a small step, if it makes the world better, it counts."

September 10

"The more I focus on making each day a day of purpose, enrichment, and fulfillment, the better I do, and the happier I am."

September 11

"I choose to live my life well, in the most positive way. I may never know all those lives I will have helped get better in my lifetime and beyond, but by helping others, I will have lived my life well."

September 12

"I make sure I'm headed in the right direction. I keep looking forward and I keep moving. I don't stop, doubt, or hesitate. I concentrate on the goal, keep my focus, stay positive, take action, and make every day count."

Self-Talk Tip #34

Having Talks with Yourself Can Change Your Day. *It Can Also Rewire Your Brain.*

Some people used to think that talking to yourself was a sign of mental illness. We now know that having a conversation with yourself can not only be *healthy*, it can also literally rewire your brain and make it better.

The problem is, most of what we say when we talk to ourselves is the same old programming, usually negative, that we were used to giving ourselves in the past. Research shows that most of our unconscious programs are the negative kind. So out of habit, we continue, unconsciously, wiring and rewiring ourselves in the same negative way.

But now imagine changing that, and having an entirely *different* conversation with yourself—using positive self-talk—the kind of conversation that tells you what you *can* do, and what *will* work. Do that like you mean it, and you can actually feel the difference physically.

Of course, while your day will usually get better, it takes more than a few talks with yourself to rewire your brain, and repetition is the key. The more often you talk to yourself with the right self-talk, the better it works. And the more you begin to rewire your brain in the positive.

September 13

"Today I choose to believe in my dreams, focus my vision, set my sights, get a clear, bright picture of my most important goal, and take a giant step forward. Today is the day I grab my goal and go for it!"

September 14

"Any doubts I might have had about myself in the past were nothing more than old programs that weren't true in the first place. Today I have faith, I have drive, I have determination, and I have belief. I can do this, and I know I can."

September 15

"Today I know what I want. I have a clear picture of my goal. I replace my doubts with determination, conquer my fears with faith, stop putting off my own success, and take action now."

September 16

"Today and every day, I choose to use the gift of choice. Each day I choose how I will spend my time, what I will think, and even what my attitude will be. I know that life is a series of choices, and I choose to make my life work right. I choose to *choose*."

September 17

"If someone were to ask me, *'Why are you here?,'* because I think about it and work to make it happen, I have an answer. I know why I am here."

September 18

"My whole world is in front of me today. I have countless opportunities. I have unlimited potential. I have an incredible attitude. I have non-stop belief. And I have *me*. It's a perfect day to love my life and go for it!"

Self-Talk Tip #35
3 Surprising Ways Self-Talk Changes Your Life

#1. When you practice the right self-talk, you set yourself up for a better future. Repeated self-talk forms new neural pathways in your brain. Those pathways form the blueprint on which your future ideas and actions will be based, and the results of those actions lead to your successes and accomplishments. Rule #1: *Your self-talk sets up your future.*

#2. Your self-talk changes how you see the world. When you're down, it's hard to believe anything can work right. When you're feeling your best, the world changes. You feel in control of your life—and when you're up, so are your successes. That's because how you see your day affects your day. Rule #2: *Your self-talk changes the world around you.*

#3. Your self-talk changes how *other* people see you. Think of a day when you were unstoppable, feeling great, and on top of the world. How did other people react to you? When your self-talk is on top, so are you. And that's how people treat you. Rule #3: *The world treats you like you treat yourself.*

September 19

"I never give up and I never give in. Instead of letting problems stop me or hold me back, I look forward to my future, I deal with the problem, and I keep moving!"

September 20

"I keep a clear picture of my goals in front of me at all times, and today especially. I see each of my goals. I believe in my ability to reach them. I take every action step I need to take. And I make sure I achieve them."

September 21

"I know that my attitude is entirely up to me. So I choose to keep my attitude up. Even when things seem down or difficult, I know the one thing I can always count on is my own bright, positive, winning attitude. No matter what, I keep my attitude up."

September 22

"Today I vote '*yes*' to success. I was born to succeed! That's how I think. That's what I do. That's how I live. And that's who I am. When it comes to success, I vote *Yes!*"

September 23

"When I want to accomplish something that's important to me, I give myself the self-talk that says, '*I have the dream. I have the goal. I have the faith. I have the drive. I have the determination. And I have what it takes to reach my goal.*'"

September 24

"My life is a joy! I have chosen to spend my time and my energies doing something that I really like, something that energizes me, and something I came here to do."

Self-Talk Tip #36
Getting Used to 'The Super You'

When you first begin practicing positive self-talk, the way you express yourself could sound strange to the people who know you. People who are unfamiliar with self-talk may wonder what's up with you, or why you're talking that way. They're not used to 'the super you.'

If you make practicing self-talk a goal, and make it part of your life, you *will* sound different. Your words and your attitudes will make some people think you've gone through an unexpected change in your personality, when you've just gone through a change in your self-talk.

When you start practicing positive self-talk, some people will love it, and they'll support you. But some may not. (Seeing you become suddenly highly positive could worry family or friends who don't understand.)

The most important thing about changing your self-talk, however, is not what someone else thinks about it. Practicing positive self-talk is about what *you* want to achieve: your goals, your attitude, how you feel each day, and living up to the individual you choose to be.

When you change your self-talk, don't worry if it sounds strange, or what other people might think. Just keep doing it. The results will speak for themselves.

September 25

"Living up to my potential is up to me. Doing great is my choice. So I never underestimate my *self* or what I can do. When it comes to what I can accomplish, and the positive good I can achieve, I never count me *out*. I always count me *in*."

September 26

"If there is a script to the story of my life, I'm writing it, I'm directing it, I'm starring in it, and I'm presenting it. It's my script, and I'm living it."

September 27

"I know that I am responsible for creating the dreams I choose to live in my life, and I am responsible for making them come true. So I visualize the dreams, follow my plan, take the next step, and make my dreams happen."

September 28

"I keep myself motivated. Each day I visualize myself reaching my goals and living my dream. I know what I want to achieve, I take action, I work my plan, I stay with it, and I get things done. I am focused, filled with energy, and very, very motivated!"

September 29

"Today I choose to turn any doubts I've had into the powerful, positive self-talk that says, *'I believe in myself! I can do this, and I know I can!'*"

September 30

"I choose to make today a wonderful, goal-reaching, purpose-fulfilling, life-enhancing day! That's my choice, and that's how I'm making today a incredible day!"

Author's Notes:
The 'Purpose' is the 'Path'

When life is busy and full of demands, what can you do to 'live your purpose' each day? The key step to staying on track is practicing being aware at all times that your purpose is also your guiding path.

When you know your purpose, you're able to begin each day with the question, *"How will I serve my purpose today?"* During that day you'll do and think many things, taking care of your responsibilities, taking care of the day, but each choice you make that day will be guided—if you're mindful of it—by your purpose.

Your purpose becomes the path or the road you walk on each day. It doesn't decide every choice for you—life still goes on in ways that often seem to have little to do with your greater purpose—but the direction you're following does. Practicing the habit of consciously following your purpose each day creates clear direction in your life; *you know why you're doing what you're doing*, and even the small things you do begin to have more value and meaning.

Then, as you go about your day, practice asking yourself at any time, *"Does this serve my purpose?"* and notice how many of your choices become focused on following that purpose. In time, following your path becomes the way you live your life.

– S.H.

158

October 1

"I know that a day is filled with many moments, with many thoughts, and many choices. The more mindful I am of my moments, my thoughts, and my choices, the better I do at reaching my goals and living for my purpose."

October 2

"I know there is a 'bigger picture' of which I am a part. And I am determined to live up to my best, fulfill my role, and do my part."

October 3

The difference between going for it and living for my purpose—or settling for 'average' and achieving little—is a choice that is mine to make. And I choose *value, a reason for being,* and living my *purpose.*

October 4

"I choose to be wise. Wisdom comes from learning from my experiences, thinking things through, always thinking before I speak, considering more points of view than my own, and never speaking without having something worthwhile to say. I choose to be wise, and it is a choice that helps me every day in many positive ways."

October 5

"I like myself already, but every day that I look in the mirror and see someone with purpose and direction, I like myself even better."

October 6

"I'm good at taking care of the present, but I also take time to practice looking far into the future. I may not control or direct everything that lies ahead, but the clearer the vision I create of my own future, the better I do at making it work."

Self-Talk Tip #37
The Importance of *'Editing'* Your Self-Talk

One of the three key steps for changing your programs is 'editing' what you think and say. Editing your self-talk is extremely important, and once you get the hang of it, it isn't difficult to do. (For all three steps to changing your programs, see Self-Talk Tip #31.)

As an example, when you're about to say or think any negative self-talk like, *"I can't remember names,"* stop yourself! Don't say it. Instead, turn it around and say, *"I'm good at remembering names. I care about people, I notice them, and I remember their names."*

That may not be true the first time you say it. But keep in mind that positive self-talk messages are showing your brain how you *choose to be*, even if you're not there yet. It you stay with it, and continue to give yourself the correct new self-talk every time the opportunity comes up, in time you will have wired that new truth into your brain, and in practice it *will* be true.

Do the same with anything you think or say that could be working against you. Change *"I'm never on time,"* to the opposite: *"I'm always on time."* Change *"I just know it's going to be another one of those days,"* to *"It's going to be a great day, and I'm going to make it that way."* Instead of telling yourself *"It probably won't work anyway!"* turn it around and say *"I can make this work. I've got this one,"* and then make it work.

Enjoy editing your self-talk! With practice you'll get good at it. In time you'll believe it. It will be you, getting to know the real you that you were meant to be in the first place.

October 7

"lt's not me, it's my programs. lf it isn't working, it's not the way l was born to be; it's the programs l received or gave to myself. lf l want to do something wonderful with my life, l can get rid of the programs that work against me, imagine the future l'd like to live, and go ahead and do it. The only thing that can stop me, is me."

October 8

"I know that true happiness comes from living my life in the very best way each day, and always keeping my purpose in front of me."

October 9

"I may come to many crosswords, and have many choices to make. But because I focus on my future, my purpose, and my goals, I always know which road to take."

October 10

"I make sure I have balance in my life. When I keep things balanced, I'm adding very important leveling to my life. When it comes to balance in anything I do, whether it is work, play, the food I eat, how I spend my time, the friends I choose, the sleep I get, or the goals I set, I use the self-talk that says, *'Everything has a right amount, and I always create the right amount of balance in my life.'*"

October 11

"I know I will become what I create in the thoughts I focus on most. When it comes to my dreams, my hopes, and my belief in myself, I choose to dream, believe I can, step forward, and make a difference. That's what I choose to create."

October 12

"How far can I see? I can see tomorrow, and see myself taking steps to reach my goals. How far can I see? I can see months and years from now, and see what I will have reached. How far can I see? I can see the future, and who I will become. How far can I see? I can see the stars."

Self-Talk Tip #38
The Right Self-Talk Is Also
Practical Self-Talk

When you first practice positive self-talk, you might think it's *too* positive—'Pollyanna positive,'—or that it might be unrealistic. But the *right* self-talk is not like that.

The right kind of self-talk is clearly positive, but it's also practical. Positive self-talk helps you see the world in a brighter way, but it also makes sure you are realistic, clear-minded and level-headed. With the right self-talk, you don't ignore problems or challenges—you deal with them. You look for solutions and find them. You don't pretend everything is rosy; you see life for what it is, but you're better equipped to handle it.

When you read the self-talk on these pages each day, at first glance it could seem like the picture of life the self-talk shows you, is too good to be true.

But read on. You'll also find self-talk that sounds something like an internal drill sergeant; it tells you to knuckle down, be responsible, work hard, take action, do it now, stop complaining, keep going, and refuse to quit. Great self-talk, and very practical.

October 13

"Most of the limits I see in front of me, are the limits I created for myself. Getting rid of my limits takes practice and the right self-talk, and I make sure my self-talk shows me what I *can* do, not what I cannot. Because I choose to see beyond my limits, my opportunities are expanding every day."

October 14

"I find the joy. I know that when I take the time to look for it and experience it, joy is all around me. And because I know joy is near, I don't just wait for it to come to me. I choose to look for the joy, I find the joy, and I feel the joy, every single day."

October 15

"I choose to think about my self-talk today, and be consciously aware of everything I think and say. Because I am mindful and aware, and because I am making sure it's the right self-talk, I'm making today work great, and my future work even better."

October 16

"I am simple, humble, and grateful in my appreciation of the life I have been given. I am also strong, determined, and powerful in what I choose to do with it."

October 17

"When I'm choosing my path in life, instead of listening to the limiting fears or disbelief of others, I see the endless possibilities that are all around me. Every time I look, I find them."

October 18

"With my incredible spirit and positive belief, I can do anything that is possible to do. This is not a world of difficulties and challenges; this is a world of endless and wonderful opportunities."

Self-Talk Tip #39

Getting Rid of 'Not Measuring Up' to Others

The idea of *'not measuring up'* is a myth. It's an idea that's based entirely on the false notion that you were designed to be like someone else. You weren't. You were designed to be you, and only you. The life you're living is *your* life, no one else's, and the only measurement of how well you're doing should be based on how well you're living up to *you*.

From this moment forward, instead of thinking about what someone *else*—or what the rest of the world thinks about you or expects from you—focus on what *you* want from you. What goals are important to you? What do *you* want to see you do? What do *you* want your purpose to be, and how will you live up to that purpose? Ultimately, that will be the only measurement that counts.

What your self-talk tells you next, and each day that follows, will be incredibly important. The self-talk you choose will define who you want to be, and what you want to do, both now, and with the rest of your life. Make sure the self-talk pictures you give yourself give you the very best picture of you. Your self-talk should never be about you 'measuring up' to the expectations of someone else. It should be your best picture of you measuring up to *you*.

October 19

"I believe in myself. I know that believing in me is a choice, so I choose to like who I am, be confident in my qualities, believe in my potential, and believe in the best outcome of anything that I do."

October 20

"Of all the roads I could walk, I choose to walk the road that helps others walk theirs."

October 21

"I have purpose and meaning in my life in both the greatest things and the smallest things I do. Whether moving a mountain or taking one breath, I have purpose."

October 22

"Each night before l go to sleep, l ask myself the question: '*What did l learn today that will help me do better tomorrow?*' When l do this, l keep myself aware of my personal growth, aware of my responsibility to myself, and aware of the endless opportunities to help me grow."

October 23

"I dream great daydreams, full of ideas and hopes and possibilities of things to come. My dreams are guideposts along the pathway of my life, and I have learned to listen to what they're trying to tell me."

October 24

"I refuse to be negative. I'm a realist. I deal with life, and I let negative things go. Anything that drains my energy or my spirit is not healthy to hold on to, and I give it no time or space in my mind or in my life."

Self-Talk Tip #40

When You Listen to Self-Talk,
Here's How to Do It

If you want to learn new, positive self-talk faster by listening to it, here's how to get the best results.

When you're getting started, it works best when you listen to the self-talk in the background, while you're doing something else. (Recorded self-talk sessions are usually from ten to twenty minutes in length.)

In the morning, play the self-talk *in the background* while you're getting ready. When you start your day with the right self-talk, you set up your day in the 'positive.'

Another time to listen is while you're doing something *physical.* Listen while you're walking, running, exercising, doing yoga, or working out. Listening while you're doing something physical is based on research that shows that our brains wire better or faster when we're physically active.

Another good time to listen to self-talk is just before you go to sleep at night. This is a great way to end the day, see yourself at your best, and get ready to take on tomorrow.

Repeat the self-talk session each day for one to three weeks on any self-talk subject you want to work on. This will give your brain the time it needs to begin wiring in the new programs you're listening to.

Join other self-talkers, and listen to your choice of self-talk every day at SelfTalkPlus.com

170

October 25

"When I think about what I can accomplish, and what is important to me in my life, instead of thinking about limitations, I think about how many positive possibilities are waiting for me."

October 26

"I keep the positive child within me alive and well. I am curious; I am interested in everything. I find life full of exciting ideas and opportunities. I'm always learning something new. I have endless dreams about my tomorrows, and I can't wait for the next day to come."

October 27

"I take the time to listen to the positive ideas I learn from others. I find good ideas everywhere. I look for ideas that increase my knowledge, my skills, and my awareness. I am open to new ideas. I learn from them, and my life always gets better because of them."

October 28

"I practice using positive self-talk every day. Because I do, I have better days, I am happier, I think better, my attitude is brighter, I deal with problems and move past them, and I open my mind to wonderful things to come!"

October 29

"Today, again, I think about the importance of living a life of service to others. The more I think about what I can do, the more I make service to others an important part of my life."

October 30

"I will never stop dreaming. I choose to dream of the amazing, unlimited possibilities in front of me. When I take the limits off, open my mind to endless possibilities, and begin to imagine myself already being there, I am, today, creating the future that one day will be mine."

October 31

"I am awake, alert, and aware, and I am conscious that I have a reason for being here, now, at this important time. I know I have a purpose and a destiny, and every day I think about the reason I am here."

Author's Notes:
Service to 'Self'— or Service to 'Others'

Each person's direction in life can be broadly grouped into one of two categories: *Service to Self*, or *Service to Others*.

The person who is always "me first" and whose conversation is dominated by words like "I" and "me" and who centers his or her life around personal attention and achievement at the expense of team or group or community achievement, lives a life of *service to self*. On the other hand, the person whose driving force is to help others do well, and who sees life as an opportunity to relate to others in a supportive way, lives a life of *service to others*.

This distinction can play a major role when you're finding your purpose. When you're looking for the answer to what you really want to accomplish in your life, ask yourself the question: *Do I choose to live my life in service to myself, or do I choose to live my life in service to others?* The answer you give can dramatically affect what you decide to do with the rest of your life.

It's my personal observation that people who live their lives in service to others—in some way helping other people do better—are the happiest, most fulfilled people on the planet. But whichever direction you choose, it is your choice.

– S.H.

November 1

"Today I choose to practice having great clarity of focus and vision. The more clearly I see things and the more vision I have, the more I understand what's really important."

November 2

"I spend no unnecessary time proving my value or worth to others. I have the strength of my own purpose, value and conviction, and I am confident within myself."

November 3

"I may listen to the advice, opinions, and ideas of others, but I listen with caution. When it comes to the choices I make about my life, I choose to listen first and last to me."

November 4

"I've got it! I have the goal, I have the opportunity, I have the tools, I have the reason, and I have the belief from others and the trust in myself. So I choose, right now to make the choice to go for it and make it work!"

November 5

"I choose to spend my time with: people who believe in me; people who trust me; people who believe in my goals; people who support me in reaching my dreams; people who accept me for who I am; people who encourage me instead of criticizing me; people who see my true potential; people who build me up, even when things are down; and people who care about me as I care about them. Today and every day, those are the people I choose to have in my life."

November 6

"When in doubt about my purpose, I ask myself two questions: *"What am I here to learn?"* and *"How can I best live my life in service to others?"* Those two questions always keep me on track."

Self-Talk Tip #41
The Better Your Self-Talk, The Higher Your Goals

The goals you set, if they're realistic, can only be as high as your expectations. And what you expect is always determined by your programs. That means that your self-talk creates the limits you put on your goals. If you want to set greater goals, you have to have the right self-talk to back them up.

Why do some people set a goal to travel the world, and actually reach the goal, while other people set a goal for something far less, or set no goal at all? It's because the person who plans to travel the world actually *sees* himself or herself doing it. That person has recorded programs that see the world-traveling goal as possible and achievable. The person without the goal is the person without the belief.

When you start practicing positive self-talk, it's a good idea to take stock of your goals. Write them down, so you know what they are. Then, after you've practiced the right self-talk for a few months, review your goals again. This time you'll find yourself resetting them higher. By reprogramming your brain to recognize what you're really capable of, your belief in yourself and your belief in your goals will have increased.

What goals could you set? What could you be capable of achieving if your internal self was completely on your side? The right self-talk will let you know that you are capable of much more, and reaching far greater goals, than you might ever have imagined.

November 7

"I always remember that my purpose is my choice, and it is up to no one else. My purpose is mine to choose and mine to live."

November 8

"I often take the time to pause, think about who I am, and the path I follow, and ask myself if I am doing what I was meant to do. Then I get a good picture of where I choose to go next, adjust my course, and take the next step forward."

November 9

"Some of the qualities l admire most are: a great attitude; compassion for others; self-confidence; positive goals; belief in the future; a willingness to work; patience; and determination to succeed. Those are qualities l admire in others. Those are qualities that create success. And those are qualities l'm building in me."

November 10

"How many purposes can I have? That's up to me. As long as all of my purposes work together, and their paths lead in the same direction—and I can fulfill them well—there is no limit to the purposes I can bring to life."

November 11

"It makes no difference how old I am at this moment, or how long it has taken me to find my purpose or to arrive at where I am today. Every day I have lived has been my preparation for now."

November 12

"I can wait for some other time, or I can find my purpose *now*. I can live a life without true direction, or I can choose now to give value to every moment I live."

Self-Talk Tip #42

Dealing With Negatives From Others

One of the things that frequently happens when you find your purpose and begin to make changes to live it out, is that other people may 'fight' your new direction. Your mate or someone close to you may not be in harmony with your change and may react in a negative way. That's fear in action, of course, but it can be tough to get past unless you arm yourself with the right attitude.

My favorite self-talk on the matter of other people's opinions is '*I never live my life based on the negative opinions of others.*' This is based on the notion that when you were born you took your first breath by yourself, and on your last day you'll take your last breath by yourself, but in between, some other people sometimes think they have the right to do our breathing *for* us. No one can breathe for you. This is your life, and it's yours to live for your reasons and your purpose, without anyone else having the right to hinder or control that purpose.

That doesn't mean that purposefully creating disharmony helps anything. But it does mean that when you search for your purpose, and especially when you find it and begin living it, do your best to gain the understanding of those around you whose own lives may be impacted (hopefully in positive ways) by *your* purpose.

November 13

"I know that there is no one stronger or more undefeatable than the person whose life is driven by unstoppable purpose. That's me. That's the person I choose to be."

November 14

"I may listen to the input I receive from others, but when it comes to following the right path for my own life, I listen to the guiding voice within me, and I take counsel with myself."

November 15

"I never get discouraged in my search to find my purpose and my path. There are many roads to travel and I know I will find the roads that are right for me."

November 16

"I find time to listen in the stillness. I listen carefully to the whispers of my soul. I listen to the quiet voice deep within me that believes in me, and helps me walk along my path. And when I listen, it is clear to me that my life has a reason, with great value and purpose, and I am not alone."

November 17

"I'm really enjoying the journey. I may not always know what is at the end of my path, but I look forward, every day, to every step I am blessed to take along the way."

November 18

"I am excited and optimistic about my future. I may not determine everything the future will bring to me, but I choose to play a major role in making it work."

Self-Talk Tip #43

Surrounding Yourself
With Success

Your brain is being wired by the people you spend your time with most. They're not trying to do that, but they are. It's the way the brain works.

Your brain is designed to record and store the messages it receives most. When you spend time with someone, especially someone you listen to and talk with frequently, *their* programs, in time, become some of *your* programs. That's why life coaches recommend you surround yourself with people you would most like to be like. Their attitudes and beliefs—their programs—will rub off on you, and get wired in.

In the same way, if you're spending a lot of time with people whose attitudes and behaviors are negative, then those programs can just as easily get wired in to your brain. If you have friends who are negative, it doesn't mean you should immediately call them and tell them dinner is off, or you won't be seeing them any more. But when choosing your friends, consider carefully who you want to have programming your brain for you.

When we were kids, our parents tried to tell us what kinds of friends we should hang around with. According to neuroscience, and how the brain gets programmed, they were probably right.

November 19

"When I let myself dream without limits, I am able to imagine the magic that is my future. I fill that future with purpose and with joy, and that is the future I am creating."

November 20

"I may not be able to determine everything about my future, but I am taking an active role in creating it, and living my own personal destiny in the most positive and fulfilling way."

November 21

"I am mindful, at all times, of the greater purpose in my life. I may live each day in a necessary way, but my life is more than each day I live."

November 22

"If there was ever a time for me to live up to my best, this is it! I am smart, capable, determined, full of ideas, filled with enthusiasm, and ready to make it work. So I have made the choice to reset my goals, believe in myself, expect the best possible outcome, get started now, and go for it."

November 23

"Because I know that I am here for a reason, I never get trapped or troubled by the small, unimportant things in life. I take care of the day, but I never let it overwhelm me."

November 24

"One of the most important choices I make is the choice not to 'fear.' Instead of being fearful, hesitant, self-doubting or uncertain, I choose to be confident, determined, self-assured, and unafraid. I know that strength is a state of mind, and I choose to be strong."

Self-Talk Tip #44
Visualization Changes Your Brain

When you visualize something clearly, your brain sees it as real. So if you want to imprint something in your brain, such as a goal you want to achieve, visualizing a clear picture of you attaining that goal will actually help your brain make it happen.

In a famous Harvard study of two groups of volunteers practicing a five-finger piano exercise, at the end of a week of piano practice sessions, both groups of volunteers showed an increase in neuronal growth in a specific region in their brain's motor cortex. This neuronal growth was the direct result of practicing the piano exercise for a period of time each day.

Here's the interesting part: one of the groups of volunteers had practiced playing the piano *only in their imagination*—without touching a piano! And they achieved results that were similar to those who had physically practiced on real pianos. Their practiced *visualization*, by itself, caused the new neurons to grow.

When you're practicing positive self-talk, make sure you're also visualizing the results you want to achieve. The more often you clearly visualize your intended result, the more your brain will see it, believe it, wire it in, act on it, and make it happen.

From *The Power of Neuroplasticity* by Shad Helmstetter, Ph.D.

November 25

"I know there are important purposes in my life.
It is my choice to find and fulfill each of them."

November 26

"When I wonder if I can, I think of all those who did. When I think I could fail, I think of all those who tried. And when I wonder if I should, I think of all those who never had the chance."

November 27

"I know that I'm not here just to be here; I'm here to make a positive difference. Every day I look for the difference I can make, and every day I add value to my life, and value to the lives of others."

November 28

"My life is not an accident, and what I do with it is important. So I think about why I'm here, and I know that what I do counts."

November 29

"My life is a gift. It is my exciting responsibility to figure out what to do with that gift. It is a wonderful gift that is mine to live, and that's exactly what I choose to do."

November 30

"To keep me mindful of my higher calling, l ask myself the questions: 'Who am l?' 'Why am l here?' 'What is my task?' and *'Am I getting it done?'* In the answers l give, l find the best of myself."

Author's Notes:
Answering the Question: *Why Am I Here?*

One of the most important questions you can ever ask is: *"Why am I here?"*

The reason the question is so important to your life is that what you think about your 'purpose' influences almost everything about you. Your beliefs about your purpose in life are, right now, affecting countless choices you're making every day, even when you're not aware you're making them.

What seems like a philosophical question that may have no real importance in everyday life, (*Why am I here?*) is, instead, connected directly to your purpose--and it affects every important choice you make, and every important goal you set. The greater and clearer your sense of purpose, the more commitment you bring to the task, the longer you stay with it, and the better you will do.

Those who find their true purpose in life rise above the issues of survival or just getting by in the everyday world. They are the individuals whose lives are exceptional. By finding your purpose you find your direction, and with that, you find greater meaning and value in your life each day. That makes discovering your purpose one of the most important goals you will ever have, and one of the most important gifts you will ever receive.

– S.H.

December 1

"The success of my day isn't just about my purpose in life. The success of my day is up to the attitude I choose that day—and I choose to have a *great* attitude *every* day!"

December 2

"I know that the greatest cure for a difficult day is knowing that what I'm doing with my life is more important that the problem I'm dealing with at the moment."

December 3

"I'm not surprised that I want to know my purpose. It comes from knowing, deep within me, that there is a reason I am here."

December 4

"Because I respect my own purpose in life, I also respect the role that others play. They have their paths, and my understanding of their paths gives me greater insight and understanding into their lives and the roads they follow."

December 5

"I know I'm on the right path when I'm helping others get better, helping myself grow, and making the world a better place."

December 6

"I create quiet in my mind. No matter what is going on around me, I practice going within myself to find that special place of peace, harmony and quiet. And from that stillness comes strength, understanding, clarity, and balance. When I practice creating quiet in my mind, I create balance in my life."

Self-Talk Tip #45
The Gold-Colored Brain

Imagine that you have a simple outline sketch of your brain. You also have three colored pens with colored ink. One pen has gray ink, one pen is neutral, and one pen has gold ink.

Imagine that every time you have a thought of any kind, you make a small mark on the picture of your brain.

If your thought is a *neutral* thought, neither positive nor negative, you make a mark on the picture of your brain with the neutral colored pen.

If it's a *negative* thought, you make a mark with the gray, dark colored pen.

If it's a *positive* or healthy thought, you mark the picture of your brain with the bright, gold colored pen.

Imagine doing that with every thought you think each day. (It's estimated that we think as many as 12,500 to 70,000 thoughts in a day, so that would be a lot of colored marks!) At the end of just one day, what color would your brain picture be? Would it be mostly bright and gold, filled with positive; would it be neutral; or would it be gray and dark, and mostly negative?

What would the picture of your brain look like at the end of a year?

And the most important question is: What color will your brain picture be at the end of your life?

From *The Power of Neuroplasticity* by Shad Helmstetter, Ph.D.

December 7

"If ever there were a moment for me to find my true self and my true meaning, that time is now. I am ready to step forward on my journey—in the most important direction of my life."

December 8

"I see life as more than the world I live in each day. I see life as learning great lessons, filled with opportunities for joy, the chance to learn to love myself and to truly love others, and the time for me to become the person I was intended to be."

December 9

"I have courage. There are times I may be uncertain or afraid, but because I choose to have courage, I replace my doubts with determination, and I change my fear to faith. And that creates my victories."

December 10

"In moving forward with my life, I have no fear. I am ready, I am prepared to do what I came to do, and I am filled with great energy and enthusiasm as I step forward into my future."

December 11

"I don't avoid the challenge, I face it. I don't fear the new, I embrace it. I don't mind the work, I enjoy it. And I don't dread the day, I thank it."

December 12

"I may be practical and realistic, but I am never afraid to dream. My dreams show me many things that I want to create in my life, and they guide me toward my future."

Self-Talk Tip #46

Living With 'Purpose' Is the Opposite of *'Putting in Time'*

We live in a culture that 'puts in time.' At work we follow the clock. At home we're limited by the time left over. Even free time, like an annual vacation, is often scheduled and rushed, and then it's back to the job and back to living for the clock again.

What is the value of all that? Usually it pays the bills and keeps us on a workable schedule of some kind, putting in time, but not necessarily going anywhere in particular.

Something odd happens to that old schedule (and it's importance) when you find your purpose and pursue it. The purpose becomes more important than the work-a-day activity that had previously consumed so many of your days. A new priority—your true purpose—comes into your life, but this one isn't bound by bosses and clocks and the endless drudgery of doing okay, but really just existing.

Purpose creates interest. Interest creates energy. Positive energy creates activity and general well-being. And no longer is life made up of 'putting in time.' Now life becomes exciting and worth living again, with each new morning heralding another day to live for your purpose. And *that* is a wonderful way to live.

December 13

"I take pride in who I am, how I think, and what I do. I am never conceited and I never have false pride, but I take honest, healthy pride in my choices to be a quality person and live a quality life. And I am proud of the person I have chosen to be."

December 14

"Having purpose in my life is not a 'now and then' thing; the value of my life is with me every day in so many ways. No matter where I am or what I'm doing, I'm mindful of who I am and why I'm here."

December 15

"The meaning of my life becomes clearer and clearer to me every day. The more I am aware of my purpose in life, and the more I seek it out, the more of it I find."

December 16

"I have focus. I practice paying attention to one thing at a time, and giving it my full attention. Because I have focus, I'm able to put all of my mental energy into anything I choose that's important to me, and I practice improving my focus every day."

December 17

"My reason for being does not have to be the same as someone else's. I listen to the ideas of others, but I know that I find my true purpose by asking myself and looking within."

December 18

"I never try to tell someone else what their purpose should be. They have their path to follow, and I have mine. I'm busy enough, just living up to the best of myself."

Self-Talk Tip #47
Believing in Your Dream

What if you have an important dream of something that you would like to do with your life, and it *could* be possible, but it doesn't *seem* possible—as though someone *else* could have that dream and make it happen, but it wouldn't work for you.

The problem is not with the dream; it's a problem of belief, and specifically with your belief in you. And that's not a bad problem to have, because 'belief' in ourselves is one thing we can change. And the best way we have ever found to change self-belief is with the right self-talk.

You could have gotten the wrong messages (programs), even thousands of them, that told what you can *not* do, or what won't work for you, or programs that caused you to not believe in yourself. But the right self-talk starting now, repeated often enough, *erases and replaces years of negative programs*—the exact programs that stopped you from believing in yourself in the first place.

There are two things you have to do: (1) Practice positive self-talk that is designed to rewire your brain with self-belief instead of self-doubt. (2) Practice seeing your 'super dreams' come to life. Write them down, literally live them in your mind, and begin to see them actually happening. If you get your self-talk right, and picture your dreams clearly every day, and refuse to give up, they will happen.

December 19

"I have been given incredible gifts. I have my life,
I have my talents, my skills, my interests my energy,
my time and my positive attitude. With those gifts,
I can do anything."

December 20

"I'm not here to live up to the expectations of
someone else. I'm here to live up to the highest
expectations of my highest self."

December 21

"I am very creative. I practice seeing things in new
and different ways. I find alternatives and look for new
solutions to any problem or opportunity. Being creative
gives me unlimited chances to grow, learn, and make
life a joyous place to be."

December 22

"I have vision. I see life beyond the moment, beyond the day, and into a future of endless possibilities. Because every day I practice having unlimited vision in anything I think or do, I am literally creating an unlimited future in front of me."

December 23

"I make good decisions. I think about my choices with intention, focus, and clarity. I think about what is right, what is best—both for me and for others—what the goal is, and what my intuition tells me. I study my choices, and I make good decisions."

December 24

"I am determined. When I have a goal and I'm doing what I know is right, I refuse to stop, give up, or give in. When I have an objective that is worthy of me and worthy of being fulfilled, I keep going until I reach it."

Self-Talk Tip #48

The Best Self-Talk for Finding Your Purpose

If there were one best self-talk phrase that you could repeat again and again, day after day, what would it be? It isn't just *one* self-talk phrase that will help you find your purpose; it's many of them, covering many areas of your life.

Here is a power paragraph of self-talk compiled from just a few of the daily self-talk phrases in this book. In reading this paragraph, it's easy to see how many different self-talk 'subjects' target the goal of finding your purpose:

"I have a purpose and a reason for being. I have many qualities, skills, and abilities—and I have all of them for a purpose. I know that I am here for a reason, and I know that it's not just to be here, but to make a positive difference. My life is not an accident, and what I do with it is important. My life is a gift. It is my exciting responsibility to figure out what to do with that gift. I do many things, and I do many things well. I am aware of improving myself, but I'm also aware of the importance of living a life of service to others. I focus every day, on the value of having purpose in my life. I look for it, I find it, and I live it."

As you can see, the self-talk in that one paragraph covers a lot of ground. Finding your purpose is not just a thought or two, it is a way of thinking that touches almost everything in your life.

December 25

"When I listen carefully, my own intuition gives me signs and signals that tell me what I want to do, what I want to achieve, and what I want to accomplish with my life."

December 26

"I'm very likable. I have a long list of positive qualities, and there are a lot of things about me to like. Right now, as I think about this, I mentally go over my list of things about me that people like. If I ever wonder about myself, I just go over my list of 'likables,' and once again, I feel great."

December 27

"Instead of finding it difficult to find something of value that I can do with my life, the more I look, the more I find that my world is filled with unlimited opportunities and possibilities. My job is to choose the best of them."

December 28

"The more I think about the contributions I can make to the world I live in, the closer I am to getting it right."

December 29

"I don't just plan to do great and incredible things with my life, I choose to create them and make them happen. I work at living a quality life, I think about what I want to accomplish, and I make sure I grow and improve in some way every day."

December 30

"I am strong, capable, and willing to do what I need to do to make my life work. I care about others, and they help me in many ways, but when it gets down to it, my success, in anything I do, is up to me. And I choose to go for it, own my success, and make my life work."

December 31

"Every day I look forward to tomorrow's new opportunities, new learning, new growth, new chances to live in service to others, and new chances to live up to the purpose I am here to fulfill.

Enjoy your purpose. It is the meaning of your life.
S.H.

You are invited to visit SelfTalkPlus.com

If you would like to join a worldwide community of positive individuals who are improving their lives by listening to self-talk daily, you are invited to visit SelfTalkPlus.com. This special self-talk community site features all of the self-talk audio programs which are certified by the Self-Talk Institute. These programs can be listened to on your laptop, tablet, smart phone, or any listening device, as often as you want, anytime you want. This is also the location to meet other self-talkers, attend special self-talk audio and video seminars, be coached by the world's best life coaches, and bring the promise, purpose, and potential of your future to life!

Join us! Visit SelfTalkPlus.com

Printed in Great Britain
by Amazon